TWENTIETH CENTURY INTE[R]
TATION OF ALL THE KING

DATE DUE			
AUG 5 '87			

DATE DUE

TWENTIETH CENTURY INTERPRETATIONS
OF
ALL THE KING'S MEN

TWENTIETH CENTURY INTERPRETATIONS OF

ALL THE KING'S MEN

A Collection of Critical Essays

Edited by
ROBERT H. CHAMBERS

Prentice-Hall, Inc.
A SPECTRUM BOOK
Englewood Cliffs, N.J

Library of Congress Cataloging in Publication Data
Main entry under title:

TWENTIETH CENTURY INTERPRETATIONS OF ALL THE KING'S MEN.

(Twentieth century interpretations) (A Spectrum Book)
Bibliography: p.
1. Warren, Robert Penn, 1905-   All the king's men.
I. Chambers, Robert H.
PS3545.A748A797   813'.5'2   77-23876
ISBN   0-13-022434-0
ISBN   0-13-022426-X pbk.

To Alice

10   9   8   7   6   5   4   3   2   1

PRENTICE-HALL INTERNATIONAL, INC., *London*
PRENTICE-HALL OF AUSTRALIA PTY. LIMITED, *Sydney*
PRENTICE-HALL OF CANADA, LTD., *Toronto*
PRENTICE-HALL OF INDIA PRIVATE LIMITED, *New Delhi*
PRENTICE-HALL OF JAPAN, INC., *Tokyo*
PRENTICE-HALL OF SOUTHEAST ASIA PTE. LTD., *Singapore*
WHITEHALL BOOKS LIMITED, *Wellington, New Zealand*

Contents

Introduction

by Robert H. Chambers

I

During the last five decades Robert Penn Warren, the man and the writer, has been continuously growing and changing. This ongoing development is hardly surprising, for it reflects the sweeping social and intellectual alterations that have characterized the time period through which the author has been living and working. Like the American people as a whole, Warren has discovered the paradox that change is the twentieth century's only genuinely verifiable constant. Accordingly, Warren's extraordinarily diverse writing career in many genres—fiction, poetry, history and biography, social commentary, and literary criticism—has been, in the main, a persistently evolving effort to come to terms with the element of change in contemporary American life and with its unsettling consequences. This is as it should be, for, as Warren himself has so aptly said, "the world changes, the totality of experience changes, and we seek a language adequate to the new experience."[1]

Because change is largely unpredictable and disrupting, it tends to breed in the individual a foreboding sense of uncertainty which, if unresolved, can lead to anxiety, dread, even to despair. The twentieth-century American, faced by a seemingly unending flux and flow in all spheres of his life, finds it exceedingly difficult, if not impossible, to define just who and what he is. But if the reality of incessant change is a dire threat, it can also be a blessing, a source of intellectual stimulation and psychological vitality. Without innovation and variety the life of the individual is stagnant, and stagnation is a very real kind of death. No matter how threatening it may be, then, change is actually required by modern man, for in it, at least potentially, lies the answer to his primary question: "Who am I?" The need for change is, as Warren has noted, "a need to dis-

---

[1] Robert Penn Warren, *A Plea in Mitigation: Modern Poetry and the End of an Era* (Macon, Georgia: Southern Press, 1966), p. 1.

cover identity—to locate oneself on the vast and shifting chart of being."[2]

To "locate oneself" through change is to attain the highest kind of "knowledge"—knowledge of self—which, according to Warren, is a fundamental "right" belonging to each individual by virtue of his existence as a human being: "...to say man's right to knowledge is simply a way of saying man's right to exist, to be himself, to be a man."[3] In Warren's view, the mere fact of life itself assumes the inviolableness of the right to seek self-knowledge:

> It assumes the right because only by knowledge does man achieve his identity. I do not mean that the mere implements of knowledge— books, libraries, laboratories, seminars—distinguish man from the brute. No, knowledge gives him his identity because it gives him the image of himself. And the image of himself necessarily has a foreground and a background, for man is in the world not as a billiard ball placed on a table, not even as a ship on the ocean with location determinable by latitude and longitude. He is, rather, in the world with continual and intimate interpenetration, an inevitable osmosis of being, which in the end does not deny, but affirms, his identity. It affirms it, for out of a progressive understanding of this interpenetration, this texture of relations, man creates new perspectives, discovers new values—that is, a new self—and so the identity is a continually emerging, an unfolding, a self-affirming and, we hope, a self-corrective creation.[4]

This eloquent statement is at once a personal testament of faith in the viability of freedom and hope and a summation of much that the writer has learned in a life-long effort to "locate" himself in an unsettled era. Warren is both formidably intelligent and formidably educated. He graduated *Summa Cum Laude* from Vanderbilt University (1925), received a master's degree from the University of California (1927), did further graduate work at Yale (1927-28), and then went on to Oxford as a Rhodes Scholar to earn his B. Litt. (1930). Yet he has found that identity, or self-knowledge, is not simply a product of the intelligence or the necessary result of a disciplined formal education. It is, rather, the constantly changing and highly subjective product of *all* of one's life experiences. The totality of experience, Warren believes, affirms human freedom by

[2]*Ibid.,* p. 2.

[3]Robert Penn Warren, "Knowledge and the Image of Man," *Robert Penn Warren: A Collection of Critical Essays,* edited by John L. Longley, Jr. (New York: New York University Press, 1965), p. 237.

[4]*Ibid.,* p. 241.

offering the individual a continually dynamic "texture of relations" which allows him to gain new perspectives, discover new values, and thereby to emerge and unfold as a free, self-determined, and "self-corrective creation." Certainly it is true that Warren himself has been a continually emerging and unfolding product of his times. More than most of us, he has exemplified that "inevitable osmosis of being" about which he has written, showing himself to be an absorber and digester as well as an analyst and critic of the experiences offered by the world around him.

Born in Kentucky near the turn of the century (April 24, 1905), Robert Penn Warren grew up during the age of optimistic liberalism which lasted well into the 1920s. Liberalism inspired in America a general spirit of confidence in man's ability to cope with life's uncertainties and to solve his pressing social problems. As the century's third decade wound to its unhappy end, however, angry voices were raised in protest against these easy assumptions. Sensing imminent social disaster, such prophets as Reinhold Niebuhr railed at illusory notions of irreversible progress toward the good life and called for a hardheaded recognition of the complexity of a world rapidly coming unglued. The Great Crash of 1929 and the Depression that followed it powerfully verified the somber warnings of Niebuhr and other spokesmen of Protestant neo-orthodoxy. By the mid-1930s it was clear that the old order of liberalism had passed and that a less optimistically naive era was in the making.

Reaching his full adulthood during this turbulent period, Warren was profoundly affected by the events of the day and by the neo-orthodox thinkers who interpreted them. Niebuhr's central concept of original sin particularly influenced the young author, whose earliest writings show an almost obsessive sense of man's fallen condition. His first published book, for example—*John Brown: The Making of a Martyr* (1929)—is a one-sided biographical depiction of an irascible sinner who foreshadows many of the troubled characters who would surface later in Warren's fiction; and *Eleven Poems on the Same Theme* (1942), his second volume of poetry, is essentially an essay-in-verse on the subject of original sin. Like Niebuhr, the young Warren felt that while man is not *simply* a sinner, corruption is, nonetheless, universal. Man is, according to this view, always in a paradoxical position. Existing at the uneasy "juncture of nature and spirit," to recall a phrase of Niebuhr's, man is both bound up and free, part of nature and yet able in part to transcend it. Consequently, he is filled with anxiety, and in order to escape the uncertainty of his situation he tends to look for a simple solution to his dilemma by emphasizing one aspect of his complex make-up over all others; and this is his sin. On the one hand, for instance, the man who is unable to cope with the demands of being free and responsible is liable to sin both by denying the reality of his freedom and responsibility and by retreating into simple animal nature, into the purely sensual side of his being. Or, on the other hand, one who is unable to accept the limitations of his humanity is liable to err by acting out of a false sense of pride, denying his limitations, and placing his confidence in himself alone. In the view of both Niebuhr and Warren, these more or less extreme positions are "unrealistic" and thus to be condemned. In Warren's novels particularly, such extremist stances are often fatal, with "salvation" or even simple survival being reserved for the fortunate few who are somehow able, against all odds, to gain a balanced, "realistic" understanding of the self and thus to accept freely both the limits and the possibilities of humanity. Jack Burden, the narrator of *All the King's Men* (1946), is one such survivor, albeit a lonely one in Warren's early fiction.

Yet, if Warren's earlier works are, in part, products of neo-orthodoxy, they are much more than that as well. While it is true that *Night Rider* (1939) and the ironically titled *At Heaven's Gate* (1943) are heavily larded with notions of human limitation, it is also true that these gloomy novels contain the seeds of the more triumphal *All the King's Men*. Never static, Warren's viewpoint has been undergoing continuous development since he began publishing in the 1920s. Like the nation as a whole, he passed through a neo-orthodox phase, but with the steady demise of neo-orthodoxy he, again like the nation, showed clear signs of moving "beyond alienation" and toward a more sustained vision of hope; Jack Burden's survival is itself a sign of such movement. As memories of the Depression and then of World War II began to fade, America settled into a period of relative security, allowing Warren and his fellow citizens to view life as more full of promise than before. Instead of dwelling on human limitation in his writing, Warren came to place increasing emphasis on the vital possibilities open to man—possibilities everywhere present, for example, in the moving and much-admired *Promises: Poems, 1954-1956* (1957), which won both a Pulitzer Prize and a National Book Award in 1958. If the America of the thirties, forties, and early fifties was primarily an anxious, troubled land, the America of the later fifties and early sixties by and large was not. Although there was by no means a euphoric return to pre-neo-orthodox liberalism, the exciting events of the time—the advance of the civil rights movement, astonishing developments in science and technology, booming economic prosperity, the coming of the Kennedys and the New Frontier, and so on — contributed to the national mood a tone of affirmation and hope. Works such as *The Cave* (1959), *Flood* (1964), and *Who Speaks for the Negro?* (1965), in addition to *Promises,* testify to the fact that Warren fully shared in the new mood.

To be sure, times continued to change. The wide-spread optimism of the late fifties and early sixties gave way to assassinations, Viet Nam, and Watergate. Once again the national mood shifted, and the many books and essays that Warren continued to produce mirrored the shift. His volumes of poetry—*Incarnations* (1968), *Audubon: A Vision* (1969), and *Or Else: Poem/ Poems, 1968-1974* (1974)—and the novel *Meet Me in the Green Glen* (1971), while hardly gloomy works, are less affirmative in tone than are their predecessors of the decade before. The joy in these recent books is more restrained, the vision less clearly hopeful. Yet joy and hope, chastened though they may appear, *are* present in these works, hinting that they are not so much historical documents as artistic reflections of the philosophical position held by Warren at the time they were written. This has, in fact, been the case with all of the author's literary efforts throughout his long, distinguished career, even in the volumes of literary criticism that have been as influential in their way as the volumes of poetry and fiction. Although, as his writings show, Warren has to a great extent "grown up" with the nation in the twentieth century, his personal development has been far more than just a barometer of the age in which he has been living. Since he is and always has been primarily an artist and not just a mirror of his particular time in history, Warren has never been simply the pawn of social and intellectual flux. Always his own man, he has remained doggedly independent as he has gone about "locating" himself in this time. And it is the combination of independence and openness to events that has been the key to his dynamic growth as a man and writer.

To the degree that he has been a product of either the nation's literary heritage or the temper of his time, Warren has continuously shown himself to be a creative product, employing the full "texture of relations" available to him to aid in his constantly unfolding creation of "new perspectives," "new values," and a "new self." Throughout his career as a writer in many genres, Warren has been concerned above all else with his personal commitment to that which he has often called "the truth of the human condition." And this is simply to say that during the exciting years of growth and change he has remained fundamentally true to himself. It could not have been otherwise, for as he has said:

The individual writer…must drive hard at his truth. He must be "committed." In whatever way he can he must drive hard to establish his own precise personal relation with the world and with literature — even at the expense of distorting history and logic more coolly considered. The writer, ultimately, makes his art from such distortion. He cannot be all things to all men, not even to truth. He can strive only to be himself—to himself.[5]

II

All the King's Men, the Pulitzer Prize winner that is Warren's finest novel, is one of American fiction's best examples of the making of art from the distortion of history.[6] Although it is obviously indebted to the rise and fall of Louisiana demogogue Huey P. Long, *All the King's Men* is largely the story of Jack Burden, wise-cracking narrator, student of history, and seeker of self-awareness.[7] The novel's intricate structure is tightly unified by the gradual unraveling of Burden's discovery of himself. As the personal recapitulation of his quest for identity, *All the King's Men* represents one of its narrator's three involved journeys into the past. In fact, Jack's dawning comprehension of the elusive meaning of his other historical excursions—the research for his unfinished doctoral dissertation on his "kinsman" Cass Mastern and his effort to "get the goods" on Montague Irwin, an effort which he calls "The Case of the Upright Judge"—is the primary subject of the narrative. Viewed in concert, the three explorations reveal that his attempts to come to terms with his "truth" have been successful. And in his success he moves beyond his predecessors in *Night Rider* and *At Heaven's Gate* to become the first of Warren's major fictional protagonists to emerge from the search for self-definition with convincing hope for a new and significant life.

Warren is no sentimentalist, however, and so Jack's eventual at-

[5]Warren, *A Plea in Mitigation,* p. 19.

[6]Unsurprisingly, its complex nature also makes *All the King's Men* one of American fiction's most "teachable" works (see Earl Wilcox's essay below).

[7]The Willie Stark-Huey Long connection generated considerable controversy at the time of the initial appearance of *All the King's Men,* as Robert B. Heilman has shown, and the controversy has raged ever since. In his 1953 introduction to the Modern Library edition of the novel and elsewhere, Warren has denied that Stark is the fictional counterpart of the Louisiana governor, but this denial has in turn been ably challenged in an essay by Ladell Payne which, like Warren's introduction and Heilman's essay, is included below in this volume.

tainment of self-knowledge comes hard, only after considerable sorrow on his part and on the parts of the other main characters. The Burden seen in most of the book is a moral failure, a sad, empty man with little cause for pride and less reason for hope. Appalled by his shallowness, he strives to hide from himself behind a protective veneer of cocky profanity. But the device fails, and Jack ends up aiming barbs in his own direction that are just as snide as those he casts at others—"Christ, Jack, you talk like a snot, Christ, you are a smart guy."[8] Beneath his cynical shield he is desperately aware of his lack of substance. Sensing that he is lost in the present, he endeavors to locate his true self by taking refuge in that part of the past represented by the agonizingly candid journal of Cass Mastern, maternal uncle of Ellis Burden, the so-called "Scholarly Attorney" who is Jack's apparent father. Yet in spite of his ready access to the "facts" of the nineteenth-century case, Jack is unable actually to *know* Cass himself—not until much later at any rate—and thus he fails to complete his dissertation. *All the King's Men* is, in part, his attempt to "look back…and try to say why" this is so.

An "exemplum" like the interpolated stories of Willie Proudfit in *Night Rider* and Ashby Wyndham in *At Heaven's Gate,* the Cass Mastern episode is one of Warren's finest sustained fictional efforts. It is a straightforward account of infidelity, betrayal of friendship, moral corruption, and overwhelming guilt, which, like a Shakespearean play-within-a-play, contains the interpretive key to the novel as a whole.[9] Its chief image is central to one's understanding of the meaning of *All the King's Men:*

> Cass Mastern lived for a few years and in that time he learned that the world is all of one piece. He learned that the world is like an enormous spider web and if you touch it, however lightly, at any point, the vibration ripples to the remotest perimeter and the drowsy spider feels the tingle and is drowsy no more but springs out to fling the gossamer coils about you who have touched the web and then inject the black, numbing poison under your hide. It does not matter whether or not you meant to brush the web of things. Your happy foot or your gay

[8]Robert Penn Warren, *All the King's Men* (New York: Harcourt Brace Jovanovich, Inc., 1946), p. 53; copyright © 1946, 1974, by Robert Penn Warren. All quotations are taken from this edition, with the permission of Harcourt Brace Jovanovich, Inc. and Eyre & Spottiswoode, and will hereafter be noted parenthetically in the text.

[9]Curiously, the Mastern story, discussed in detail below by Beekman W. Cottrell, was deleted entirely by the original British publishers of *All the King's Men* (Eyre and Spottiswoode, London, 1948), who studiously ignored its integral centrality.

wing may have brushed it ever so lightly, but what happens always
happens and there is the spider, bearded black and with his great
faceted eyes glittering like mirrors in the sun, or like God's eye, and
the fangs dripping.   (200)

This Bergmanesque spider-God betrays Warren's view that the
facts of mutual limitation and complicity are the principal definers
of the human condition. Man, as the author depicts him, is simply
unable to escape the hard realities of his uncertain, corrupt existence and thus is liable to blunder unwittingly into "the web of
things," thereby unleashing all manner of woeful consequences beyond his control. Bound inevitably by his innate corruption, he can
hope to transcend it only through conscious recognition of the ab-
soluteness of his complicity. Acknowledgement of his responsibility
in brushing the web is, according to Warren, man's sole route to that
genuine selfhood which is his freedom. Without such acknowledgement, spiritual and psychological liberation are impossible; with it,
freedom becomes a likelihood. In Cass Mastern's case liberation is
the welcome reward for years of contrition. Having lived and suffered long enough to realize "that the world is all of one piece,"
he dies in the awareness that he is at last being delivered from "the
common guilt of man." The final words in Cass's journal are in
thanks to God, who "in His mercy has spared me the end." (199)

"But how could Jack Burden, being what he was, understand
that?" (200) How indeed? Unlike Cass Mastern, he had not yet (at
the time) attained the degree of insight needed to comprehend the
complex interrelatedness of men and events. To him

> the world then was simply an accumulation of items, odds and ends of
> things, like the broken and misused and dust-shrouded things gathered
> in a garret. Or it was a flux of things before his eyes (or behind his
> eyes) and one thing had nothing to do, in the end, with anything else.
> (201)

Totally unaware of the "truth" of complicity, Jack was, of course,
insufficiently experienced to understand anything about Mastern —
his self-chosen suffering, his vision of the world's oneness, or, above
all, his prayerful acceptance of the "Justice of God." Depressed by
his failure, the student of history had laid aside Cass's journal and
entered upon one of those strange periods of escape known to him
as a "Great Sleep," his first excursion into the past concluding in
a dreamlike flight into oblivion. The researcher's reward was not the
insight he craved, but an increase in his already profound sense of

anxiety. As Jack tells the reader, "It [the research] had not been successful because in the midst of the process I tried to discover the truth and not the facts." (167) Having determined not to commit that error again, he pursued his second historical foray—"The Case of the Upright Judge"—in such an impersonal and objective manner as to make it "a sensational success." (203) In following the orders of "Boss" Willie Stark, self-made governor of the state, Jack concentrated solely upon "the facts" of the Judge's case, leaving "the truth" to fend for itself. Consequently, he ferreted out the concrete data that would destroy Irwin, the man who was actually his father, and shatter the lives of most of the other characters in *All the King's Men*. Jack sought concrete results, and he got them.

Ironically, Burden had entered upon his second research project with the intention of substantiating the Judge's fine reputation. Not yet the confirmed nihilist he was to become, he believed that Irwin's widely revered integrity would stand as a righteous refutation of Willie Stark's primary article of political faith: "Man is conceived in sin and born in corruption and he passeth from the stink of the didie to the stench of the shroud." (54, 167) Stark, convinced that "there is always something"—i.e., something evil in the back room—had once told Jack, "I went to a Presbyterian Sunday school back in the days when they still had some theology, and that much of it stuck...I have found it very valuable." (358) The "success" of Jack's investigation, far from refuting such cynicism, served only to underscore the apparent truth of Willie's confidence in universal depravity. By exposing the "facts" of the Judge's murky past—years earlier, when serving as Attorney General of the state, Irwin had taken a large bribe, violated his position of public trust, and caused a man to commit suicide—the student of history, immersed in his logical objectivity, had brushed "the web of things" to such an extent that neither he nor anyone else in the novel could long remain untouched:

> ...And Masters [a corrupt politician] is dead now, as dead as a mackerel...And Callahan [another politician] is not dead but he has wished he were, no doubt, for he used up his luck a long time back and being dead was not part of it. And Adam Stanton is dead now, too, who used to go fishing with me and who lay on the hot sand in the hot sunshine with me and with Anne Stanton. And Judge Irwin is dead, who leaned toward me among the stems of the tall gray marsh grass...and said, "You ought to have led that duck more, Jack. You got to lead a duck, son." And the Boss is dead, who said to me, "And make it stick."
> (54)

As he sarcastically notes, "Little Jackie made it stick, all right." In doing so he lowered his own already low estimation of human nature nearly to the vanishing point. Having learned from his second historical journey that "badness" is seemingly the basic human fact, Jack was on the verge of accepting Stark's bleak view of existence. With his faith in the integrity of Judge Irwin in ruins, he had only his pure image of Anne Stanton to keep him from yielding to Willie's dark philosophy. Yet even this last outpost of innocence proved to be unreliable. Jack's lingering belief in virtue was shattered by his discovery that Anne had become the mistress of Willie Stark. What is more, Jack himself, having once acted "nobly" and thereby lost his sole opportunity to marry Anne, was consumed by the thought that he had somehow handed her over to Willie.[10] "So," he observed, "my nobility (or whatever it was) had had in my world almost as dire a consequence as Cass Mastern's sin had had in his." (315) Unable to cope with the horror of this "fact," Jack, unsurprisingly, once again found himself in hard flight from reality. This time, though, his temporary escape led to "the dream" that would allow him to resign himself (if only for a while) to the complexity of human relationships:

> That dream was the dream that all life is but the dark heave of blood and the twitch of nerve...It was bracing because after the dream I felt that, in a way, Anne Stanton did not exist. The words *Anne Stanton* were simply a name for a peculiarly complicated piece of mechanism which could mean nothing whatsoever to Jack Burden, who himself was simply another complicated piece of mechanism...That dream solves all problems.   (329)

Having bathed in the soothing waters of determinism and thereby been purged of all lingering notions of responsibility, Jack emerged a new man, free, strong, self-sufficient: "I did not think that I would ever have to envy anybody again, for I was sure that now I had the secret knowledge, and with knowledge you can face up to anything, for knowledge is power." (332) A total nihilist now, Burden found a liberating sense of security in his new belief that the incomprehensible God of Cass Mastern had been superseded by the so-called "Great Twitch," the naturalistic deity of pure and simple reaction. Moreover, Jack's discovery also brought with it an impres-

[10]When, years earlier, Anne was naked and alone with Jack in his bedroom, he did not take her sexually because "it wouldn't be right." Anne's innocence, since destroyed by her liaison with Stark, had overwhelmed him at the time. Had Jack acted less "nobly" then, their families would have arranged for the marriage of the young couple, and "all might have been different."

sion of intellectual superiority, for he alone appeared to understand the true nature of the human situation. Even Willie Stark, the man who had everything, including Anne Stanton, had everything "except the thing I had, the great thing, the secret." (334) While others might have dimly perceived the presence of the Great Twitch, only Jack actually knew that it "was all."

This newborn "innocence" of Burden's was, however, to be short-lived, for his false sense of security was rooted in an illusion roundly repudiated by Robert Penn Warren. As noted above, Warren has taught throughout his career that knowledge alone is a poor savior. In a meditative essay on the merits of Shakespeare, Slim Sarrett, an anxious but intelligent character in *At Heaven's Gate*, states the author's position clearly and succinctly:

> Bacon wrote: Knowledge is power. Bacon was thinking of knowledge of the mechanisms of the external world. Shakespeare wrote: Self-knowledge is power. Shakespeare was thinking of the mechanisms of the spirit, to which the mechanisms of the external world, including other persons, are instruments. In other words, Shakespeare was interested in success. By success, he meant: self-fulfillment.[11]

Since, in Warren's view, not just knowledge, but self-knowledge is power, Burden's naive elation over his "dream" was even more superficial than his earlier philosophical positions. As one would expect, then, events were to show him that simple reaction—the Twitch—was not "all"; and in this further revelation would lie the path to that knowledge of himself which would eventually be his redemption. Having sunk to both a spiritual and an intellectual nadir with his espousal of determinism, Jack had only one direction left in which to move—toward personal definition and hope. Each of the steps to be taken in this direction involves him in a dramatic confrontation with one of his three "fathers"—Judge Irwin, Willie Stark, and Ellis Burden.[12] Together, the trio of confrontations serve to shatter Jack's nihilism by revealing that the relationships between men and events are far more complex than the simplistic concept of the Great Twitch would imply.

From the Judge's suicide and the subsequent disclosure that Irwin, and not the Scholarly Attorney, was his literal father, Burden learned that appearance and reality are not necessarily identical.

[11]Robert Penn Warren, *At Heaven's Gate* (New York: Random House, 1943), p. 196.

[12]For varying perspectives on Jack's symbolic father-quest, see the essays below by Jonathan Baumbach, Norton R. Girault, and Robert C. Slack.

Yet if the lesson surprised him, it seemed hardly to scratch his shell of cynical indifference…at least not for a time. Pondering his own obvious responsibility for the Judge's death, Jack coolly decided: "Well, I had swapped the good, weak father for the evil, strong one. I didn't feel bad about it…There was no use trying to probe my feelings about them, for I had lost both of them." (375) Burden's indifference, though, was only apparent. Clearly, the entire affair had shaken him to the roots. When told that he was the sole heir to the Judge's estate, Jack—"the blameless instrument of justice"— burst out laughting, but his laughter quickly turned to tears:

> I found that I was not laughing at all but was weeping and was saying over and over again, "The poor old bugger, the poor old bugger." It was like the ice breaking up after a long winter. And the winter had been long.   (376)

The death of Judge Irwin, therefore, signaled the beginning of his son's gradual process of rebirth, of his "self-location." Like the breaking of the winter ice, it cracked the narrator's emotionless facade, making possible the penetration of a second lesson—that man is not inevitably subject to the mindless whims of the Twitch. The medium of this revelation was Jack's surrogate father, Willie Stark, who late in *All the King's Men* is depicted as having undergone a complete change of heart in the wake of the swelling sorrow around him. Stunned by a disabling and ultimately fatal football injury to his son Tom, the "Boss" abruptly decided to clean up his shady political deals, forsake his mistress (Anne Stanton), and return to his pious, forgiving wife Lucy. Ironically, in the midst of his radical reformation, Willie was murdered by Adam Stanton, who "wouldn't be paid pimp to his sister's whore." (413) Stark's dying words to Jack, the most important spoken by him, are vital to an understanding of the entire novel. Not only do they reveal the depth of his own spiritual rehabilitation—he was able to sympathize with and forgive his murderer—they also deliver a mortal blow to the philosophy of naturalistic determinism:

> …"Why did he do it to me?…I never did anything to him…He was all right. The Doc."
> I waited, but it began to seem that he wasn't going to say any more. His eyes were on the ceiling and I could scarcely tell that he was breathing. Finally, the eyes turned toward me again, very slowly, and I almost thought that I could hear the tiny painful creak of the balls in their sockets. But the light flickered up again. He said, "It

might have been all different, Jack…You got to believe that…And it might even been different yet," he whispered. "If it hadn't happened, it might—have been different—even yet."   (424-425)

And for Jack Burden it *would* be different. The violent deaths of his literal and surrogate fathers were the agents of his spiritual "self-location." Having learned the value of love from Judge Irwin and the power of will from the last words of Willie Stark, Jack was freed from being either nihilist or escapist. Liberated from the felt need to be cynically detached, the former "objective" observer could now understand the necessity for his personal involvement in the world's oneness. Although that oneness bound him inevitably and inextricably to the world's evil—hence his acknowledgment of kinship with the repulsive Tiny Duffy, the new governor whose insinuations to Adam Stanton about the affair between Adam's sister and Boss Stark had led to the latter's death—it also freed him to experience the comfort of human relationships. Accepting his own failings, he could accept the inadequacies of others as well. No longer convinced of his intellectual superiority, he was now prepared for reconciliation with the woman he loved, the mother he had loathed, and the only father he had left.

Before marrying Anne Stanton, Jack returned to his childhood home at Burden's Landing where he found his mother alone for the first time in many years. Shocked by the sudden death of Judge Irwin, the only man she had genuinely loved, she had abruptly sent away the last of a long line of gigolos. Jack's unwitting betrayal of his father had, therefore, unexpectedly made possible the regeneration of his mother; as he noted, "by killing my father I had saved my mother's soul." (455) Moreover, this creation of "goodness" out of "badness" was to have a snowballing effect. For example, when asked by Mrs. Burden why the Judge had shot himself, Jack implied that the suicide resulted not from political chicanery, but from bad health. In this tacit recognition of the pre-eminence of "truth" to "the facts" lay the proof of his own redemption:

> I had given my mother a present, which was a lie. But in return she had given me a present, too, which was a truth. She gave me a new picture of herself, and that meant, in the end, a new picture of the world. Or rather, that new picture of herself filled in the blank space which was perhaps the center of the new picture of the world which had been given to me by many people, by Sadie Burke, Lucy Stark, Willie Stark, Sugar-Boy, Adam Stanton. And that meant that my mother gave me back the past. I could now accept the past which I had

before felt was tainted and horrible. I could accept the past now because I could accept her and be at peace with her and with myself.
(458)

With his acceptance of the past, Jack was also able to reconcile himself to Ellis Burden, the sad, Bible-quoting "old man who was once married to my mother." His one-time contempt for his last father having turned to compassion, the narrator had taken the Scholarly Attorney into his home and even consented to write down the dying old man's religious thoughts, one of which expresses the central meaning of *All the King's Men:*

> The creation of man whom God in His foreknowledge knew doomed to sin was the awful index of God's omnipotence. For it would have been a thing of trifling and contemptible ease for Perfection to create mere perfection. To do so would, to speak truth, be not creation but extension. Separateness is identity and the only way for God to create, truly create, man was to make him separate from God Himself, and to be separate from God is to be sinful. The creation of evil is therefore the index of God's glory and His power. That had to be so that the creation of good might be the index of man's glory and power. But by God's help. By His help and in His wisdom.   (462-463)

Recalling the hopeful epigraph from Dante that opens the novel — *"Mentre che la speranza ha fior del verde"*[13] — this brief, explicit theological statement indicates the complexity of Warren's view of the notion of original sin. According to that view, man's "sinfulness" is not only the sign of his alienation from God and from himself, it is also the source of human definition, "glory," and "power." Paradoxically, although sin may imprison one in evil and guilt, it makes possible individual freedom and "goodness" as well. Indeed, Warren implies that the tension between these opposing possibilities *is* the human condition. Consequently it is only through perceiving and acknowledging the reality of both that one is able to approach that genuine knowledge of self which is potentially redemptive.

As *All the King's Men* shows, Jack Burden has neared this kind of saving self-knowledge. Having, at one time or another, assumed many positions along the philosophical spectrum (from naive idealism to equally naive mechanism), he emerges from his quest balanced and whole, tacitly assenting even to the truth of the Scholarly Attorney's theology, though, to be sure, "in his own way." (463) Like Ishmael in *Moby-Dick,* Jack mediates between destructive

---

[13]Taken from Canto III of "Purgatorio," in *The Divine Comedy,* the line has been translated by Lawrence Grant White as "so long as hope stays green."

extremes—between Adam Stanton, the "man of idea," and Willie Stark, "the man of fact" (462)—and survives as a result.[14] His once fragmented psyche having been put together, he becomes one of the king's men who endures the Fall. What's more, Jack, unlike Humpty-Dumpty, actually profits from the experience.[15] Understanding his past, the spider web of human involvement, and himself, he concludes his novel with a hint that soon he plans to complete his other book—the life of Cass Mastern. He now faces the future with hope and is prepared to go forth "into the convulsion of the world, out of history into history and the awful responsibility of Time." (464)

[14]Jack's implication that Adam and Willie represent "the terrible division of their age" is discussed below in detail by Jerome Meckier and James C. Simmons.

[15]For a discussion of the richness implicit in the novel's title, see the essay below by James Ruoff.

Melpomene as Wallflower; or,
the Reading of Tragedy

by Robert B. Heilman

Everybody knows that the eighteenth century marked, in English literature, the disappearance of tragedy and the rise of the novel. As neoclassicism set in, something happened to the tragic sense, a something which included the growth of the scientific attitude and the subtle adulteration of the Christian view of experience—in, for instance, the pressure of prudential upon transcendental values. There is a weakening of the grasp of man's inner contradictions and complexities upon which tragedy, and for that matter the highest comedy, depends. In its direction the novel was social, even sociological; its concern was less the troubled man than troubles between men—if it rose to a consideration of troubles at all—and between men who were whole and easily catalogued: Joneses, Allworthys, Brambles, Evelinas, Elizabeth Bennetts, Micawbers, Beckys, Grantleys, Patternes. For literature, the content of experience became stabilized at that level, and on that level some men of letters are still content to remain. But tragic experience, however much enlightenment we have, keeps stabbing at our imaginations: the novel, irregularly, tentatively, and yet with a kind of determination, has kept probing and thrusting toward the tragic awareness of life which drama has never recovered: half the history of English fiction is the quest for tragedy. George Eliot, overly condescended to now, begins to cut back into the inner man; the older Hardy goes further; James, Conrad, and Joyce lay hold of inner obscurities, parts that do not match; Faulkner seizes upon disruptive urgencies and intensities. Robert Penn Warren's *All the King's Men* adds a chapter to the history of the recovery of tragedy.

"Recovery" is probably the right word, for Elizabethan, and possibly Greek, tragedy has made a mark on *All the King's Men.*

"Melpomene as Wallflower; or, the Reading of Tragedy" by Robert B. Heilman first appeared in the *Sewanee Review* 55 (1947); 154-66. Copyright 1947 by the University of the South. Reprinted by permission of the editor and the author.

Shakespeare won the pit, and this novel is a best seller, which is to say that there is a level of dramatic tension more widely accessible than one expects in the philosophic novel. The plot involves public figures, but the record is finally of the private agony (as with Macbeth and Oedipus). The author begins with history and politics, but the real subject is the nature of them: Warren is no more discussing American politics than *Hamlet* is discussing Danish politics. Then there are the chronic intra-family confrontations and injuries, the repercussions of generation upon generation, as with Hamlet and Orestes—a type of situation which, it may be observed in passing, Aristotle praises. As with the older tragedy, all this can look like steaming melodrama if one wants to stop at the deed as deed and simply forget about meanings. But as in the older poetic tragedy there is, beneath all the explicitnesses, a core of obscure conflicts, of motives partly clouded, of calculations beset by the uncalculated, of moral impasses in which both action and inaction may damn, and Oresteian duty be Oresteian guilt.

All the King's Men is the tragedy of incomplete personalities whose interrelationship is rooted, in part, in the impulse to completeness—in the "agony of will." Anne Stanton cannot find it in the uncertain, unfocused young Jack Burden, sardonic in a detachment closer to alienation than objectivity; by contrast the rude, better-directioned power of Willie Stark acts compellingly upon her. Dr. Adam Stanton, the man of idea, cut off, driving himself with ascetic, self-destructive violence, seeks, though apparently acting unwillingly, a liberating public deed which allies him with Willie Stark, the man of fact—the split between whom and himself, as symbolic modern characters, provides the explicit philosophic groundwork of the story. Jack Burden, the narrator, rootless, shrewd, speculative, but unintegrated, lacking so to speak, a personality, gives his life an appearance of personal form by his close attachment to Willie, who has cohesion and aim and genius for the action that organizes and excites—and that still calls up slow questions, questions which Jack, in evidence of his never quite blotted out iota of grace, always keeps asking. Everybody's needs are ironically summed up in the grotesque gunman, Sugar-Boy, the stutterer who loves Willie because Willie "can talk so good." Willie completes the others, whose need is a centering and a commitment; but Willie cannot complete himself. In a complex of polarities that are structurally important throughout the novel, Willie also seeks completion in them—an identification with idea and tradition, and with the asker of questions in whom he senses an entryway into a

realm beyond facts. For in Willie, the man of fact, there is the paradox of action; action completes and yet is incomplete; action is
necessary but is never pure; action begs to be undertaken but imposes its conditions. Adam cannot sufficiently accept the conditions
of action, and Willie cannot sufficiently escape them. But if Willie
cannot save himself from his gift, he can, as is needful in tragedy,
understand himself; the man of action becomes the self-critic in
action when, in every phase of the hospital drama, he actually, if
not overtly, repudiates his working half-truths.

A plurality of heroes is one symbol of a riven world. There are
in Warren's novel other partial men; there is especially Jack, whose
story, he says, is Willie's story: he is the riven world which produces
Willie and serves him and yet always keeps a last thin aloofness
from him, and which through him comes to a possibly saving understanding—the note of hope, of spiritual discovery, which completes
tragedy. Jack is a scarred Ancient Mariner telling what happened
and what he learned; he stubbornly tells it in a style which recreates
things as they were to him, without benefit of the exceptions he
might not make in his maturity.

I have stressed Mr. Warren's belonging to the tragic tradition
because his book has brought into focus a very disturbing situation—
our sheer incompetence to read tragedy. A large number of critics
have beaten Mr. Warren around the ears and cried that he should
have written a political melodrama. He woos a long-neglected Melpomene, and is told he should be doing a carmagnole with an up-
to-date Clio. He tries to give his readers the universal in the unique
form which is the individual work of art, and they bawl at him for
not sticking to social platitudes. He gives them metaphysics, and
they call pettishly for sociology. Well, he does give them some social
documentation, all right, but he gives it to them the hard way: he
pictures for them the spiritual condition—the decline of tradition,
the loss of an integrating force, the kind of split—which results in
Willie-as-hero; he makes it still harder for them by pointing out the
kind of greatness Willie had to have to be to a society what he was.
Warren says, I take it, that a universal complement has to be a little
more than a melodrama villain. But they do not want understanding
—because it involves the pain of self-scrutiny? They know in advance that Willie, insofar as he is Humpty, is a bad egg who ought
to have had a fall; we should simply and happily hoot him. And
feel ever so warm a glow inside. But we can get a warm glow from
liquor or likker, and some prefer chemical analysis.

Most of the daily and weekly reviewers who tell America what to

read still have the simplified view of *belles lettres* deriving from the
eighteenth century. Of some two score of them whose reviews of
All the King's Men I have been able to see, precisely two have a
complete grasp of the work as tragedy: Henry Rago in *Commonweal*
and Brainard Cheney in the Nashville *Banner,* both of whom do
brilliant analyses. Four others come close: Victor Hamm in the
Milwaukee *Journal,* Paul Engle in the Chicago *Tribune,* Granville
Hicks in the *American Mercury,* and Lee Casey in the *Rocky Moun-
tain News.* Surely these publications would not come to mind as the
first six most likely sources of critical light in America. But by their
diversity and distribution they establish the public intelligibility
of Mr. Warren's novel; it is clearly not a work for club members
only. Besides these six, about fourteen—in all, a little less than half
of those I have seen—recognize that the novel is of philosophic
dimensions. George Mayberry of the *New Republic* and James
Wood of the *Saturday Review* read the book very intelligently; but
the philosophic insight of others is often neither large nor secure.
Most reviews are laudatory, some of them grudgingly, and others
clearly uncertain why. The *Daily Oklahoman* headlines its review,
"Nothing To Do But Like This Gay Old Cuss." From such a journalistic cradle, presumably typical, it is, paradoxically, not too far to the
mature journeyman critics, a dozen or so of them, who provide the
real problem for discussion. They are the ones who fear that Mr.
Warren fails to show the dangers of dictatorship, or who outright
accuse him of defending or aiding fascism. If these were all journalistic hillbillies, one could shed a tear for the darkness of the
underbrush and forget it; but they furnish part of the candlepower
of some of the stronger fluorescent lights in Megalopolis—the New
York *Times, PM,* the *Nation,* and the papers that subscribe to John
Cournos and Sterling North. Further, Fred Marsh of the *Herald
Tribune* fails so completely to understand the book that he finally
hypothesizes that it may be "intended only as melodrama in modern
prose."

It would be easy to compile a florilegium of critical quaintnesses.
Only two reviewers, for instance, indicate awareness that the man-
agement of the religious theme at the end is more than a pious post-
lude. The *New Yorker* and the Chicago *Sun* both regard Jack Burden as an interloper; *PM* and Sterling North regard the Cass Mastern
episode, which is of high structural importance as an intrusion. Most
of the commentators on style should go to Henry Rago of *Commonweal* for a lesson on the quality and functional role of the style. Of
three reviewers who use the word *slick,* only Robert Gorham Davis

of the *Times* adduces evidence—two sentences, both of which, he fails to realize, are indications of the attitude of Jack Burden; the second he particularly mistreats by lifting it, without explanation, from a bitterly ironic context. But what is one to think of reviewers' sense of style in general when he can find applied to Mr. Warren's writing two such beautifully irreconcilable judgments as those of Fred Marsh in the *Herald Tribune* and Laban C. Smith in the Chicago *Sun?* The former's words: "elaborately stylized prose (since nobody ever either talks or writes like this)." Mr. Smith's comment on figures of speech: "most of them very familiar if not trite, and the full development of these figures and their repetition frequently corrupts...a strong and intelligent style."

But the heart of the matter is this: why can so few critics read tragedy, and what are the implications of this disability of theirs? In the muddling over *All the King's Men* we can see several main tendencies, overlapping and not always properly distinguishable; perhaps they are all facets of a central cultural phenomenon. As a group the reviewers exhibit certain habits of mind that have been familiar since the eighteenth century—habits which appeared as tragedy began to disappear and which, as long as they are general and uncorrected, are, without necessarily intending to be so, hostile to tragedy and to the insights made possible by the tragic sense. Perhaps the presence of these habits means simply the absence of the tragic habit of mind. Then the novelist faces the hard task of creating it for himself. The habits against which he will have to contend are the Puritanical, the sentimental, the scientific, the social-topical, and the lotos-eating or slothful.

The Puritanism that one finds in the reviews of *All the King's Men* is of the pale, literal, unhand-me-sir kind that, when Troy is falling, complains of, or even rises to a certain vice-squad petulance against, naughty words on the wall. Eunice Ross Perkins grieves, in the Macon *Telegraph*, that there is "no really fine" woman in the book and that Mr. Warren has not caught sight of the really very nice things in the South. The same obtuseness appears in two ecclesiastical organs, with which *Commonweal* is an encouraging contrast: Harold C. Gardiner in *America* abuses the book as blasphemous and immoral, and Daniel Poling in the *Christian Herald* regrets that Mr. Warren "goes into the gutter." Mr. Warren is trying to tell them about Troy, and they look for The Story of the Good Little Boy. A man's search for truth is too tough substance for these sentimental hand-me-downs from a simpler day. A cousin of theirs, Ethel Dexter of the Springfield *Republican,* wonders how women can really fall in love with such a fellow as Willie. These are familiar cries for familiar pluckings of the heartstrings. Give the cries a political twist, and they become demands for praise of reigning dogmas, and caveats against inquiry into underlying truths.

The scientific mind turns from esthetic problems to the provenience of the book, the man behind the book, the book's effect on society, etc.: a perverse factuality trespasses on the domain of the imagination. Certain reviewers cannot separate Willie Stark from Huey Long; some actually fear that Mr. Warren is not *biographically* accurate. Such minds cannot distinguish fact and fiction, the point of departure and the imaginative journey; they cannot realize that a few biographical facts are merely, and can be no more than, an alterable design for a mold into which the artist pours such dramatic body and such values as his insight permits. How can these people read Shakespeare? Some of them, self-consciously sharp, scream "special pleading"; Sterling North and Robert Davis consider the novel a personal apologia, an apologia, Davis says outright, for having edited *The Southern Review* at Louisiana State University. It may be remarked parenthetically that Mr. Davis's criterion, if applied with any sort of consistency at all, will deprive most universities of their faculties and most money-making periodicals of their reviewers. What is of critical interest, however, is not Mr. Davis's squinting detectivism, but the pseudoscientific, psychology-ridden cast of mind, with which he is obviously well satisfied, that makes it literally impossible for him to read and understand the literary evidence. He cannot tell what the story says; he simply cannot grasp the author's detachment and integrity.

This category of incompetence overlaps the next, where we find the science-and-society frame of mind. Historically, this kind of reader represents the main tradition of the English novel, which finds its tensions in social patterns, in problems of relationship in society rather than in the individual. But societies change, and with the evolutionary friction the social becomes the topical. To us, in our day, the social appears as the real, and atmospheric pressures tend to convince the writer that literature ought to be an adjunct of societal reordering. Now this concept, if taken as profoundly as possible, could accommodate high literature; Mr. Warren is concerned with society: his very subject is the split personality of an age. But the self-conscious practitioner of social consciousness does not want such radical investigations; he has already done the diagnosis, and all he wants is a literary pharmacist to make up the prescribed vitamin and sulfa pills.

The social-topical critics, bound by their inflexibly applied theory of literature, cannot read the individual work. But there are degrees of subtlety among them. Granville Hicks, as I have already said, gives so sensitive an account of *All the King's Men* that he does not belong with the table pounders at all—except for one small point: he notes Shaw's and Steffens' insistence on changing a corrupt society, and adds that Mr. Warren says nothing of socialism. That is all; yet it suggests that Mr. Hicks wants the novel to do something which is hardly in its province. But he holds to his dogma with such tact that he is not blinded to the goodness of what has been done. It is quite a step down, therefore, to Saxe Commins, who in the Cleveland *News* pays formal tribute to Mr. Warren's various skills but goes on to express regret for Mr. Warren's indifference to Negroes and "the people who should be the concern of the state." Mr. Commins' social concern is familiar: he wants a conventional conflict developed by standardized dramatic symbols; he wants the novelist to be a one-man pressure group instead of a man of tragic vision. So, dogma-bound, he gravely warns that the novel serves to glamorize the man in the "bullet-proof limousine" and thus to "invite disaster." Diana Trilling of the *Nation* imagines that Mr. Warren is defaming Hegel's relativism and hence gets things so out of focus that she perpetrates an extraordinary series of misreadings. She calls Jack Burden's Twitch theory "embarrassingly maudlin"—and completely misses Jack's repudiation of the theory. She says that Jack's "moral awareness" is of "low quality" and that he has a fine eye but "no equivalent gift of inward vision." She utterly misses his long search for truth, his reflectiveness, his later understanding of Cass Mastern, his insight into the Adam-Willie cleavage. What must a man do to exhibit vision? Declaim the Bill of Rights? Mrs. Trilling thinks the hospital is meant to establish Willie as a benefactor and that Mr. Warren approves of Willie because Willie is Jack's "hero." Even a strong commitment to liberal dogma seems hardly sufficient to explain, in a justly distinguished professional critic of fiction, such gross over-simplification of what a book says.

Dawn Powell gives the readers of *PM* little more than flippancies; but she closes with the warning that increasing regard for the strongman legend may be paving the way "for a really successful Willie Stark." Sterling North's purely literary comments are too genuinely stupid to warrant mention; what he lacks in insight he makes up in insolence and malevolence. But is he, in his political and moral judgments, really the honest barbarian he looks? Beats there a heart of gold below the red neck? Or is he the slicker in the backroom who knows what the customers want? Are there pleasant little pills in the innocent, downturned palm?

Diana Trilling, Dawn Powell, and Sterling North—a pretty bedful. And when we find the somewhat primly schoolmasterish Robert Davis's head on the same pillow—he assures us that Warren is playing Parson Weems to Huey's Washington—the picture has a wonderfully satisfying completeness. For what do they all do but pull the covers up over their heads and refuse to listen to the real warnings about the society they are so preciously and loudly concerned about? They have taken the symptom for the disease, and they want the symptom denounced; out, out, dark pimple. When an artist takes the symptom and traces it to radical causes— and when he even shows the kind of consciousness that nourishes the causes and with a severely disciplined hopefulness shows a possibly saving alteration in that consciousness—they mistake him for a germ carrier. The artist proceeds from the region to the civilization, and from the civilization to the dangers of disintegration implicit in human life; this is tragedy; but they cannot read it, and in their confusion they are as complacent as if they were protecting Humpty down there under the covers.

Before we turn out the light and tiptoe away from this dormitory and its fantasies, we need to note that, aside from missing what is in the book, Mr. Davis prescribes a formula for contemporary fiction: that "we fight men like Long with the utmost resolution...to preserve...free, open, pluralistic societies...." One may doubt whether *Macbeth* would have been improved if it had been conceived as a recipe for the curtailment of royal abuses. Mr. Davis makes the old confusion of citizen and artist; but, what is far worse, he is apparently bent on imposing upon the artist a topicality, and a predetermined point of view, which must dull and destroy his insight. It is dangerous to read badly; but it is a terribly serious matter when an elite itself—I refer to most of the critics I have quoted—when this elite, as if moved by a devastating self-distrust, calls for easy propaganda in place of the difficulties of tragedy. It is easy to hate a villain; and it is usually the groundlings who want life reduced to a manageable melodrama. What if all artists give in?

In many of these readers of *All the King's Men* there is plain slothfulness—not as a personal vice but as public habit which appears to have grown since the eighteenth century, to have been nourished upon and in turn to have insisted upon, a relatively simple, one-dimensional literature. Not that there has not been difficult, complex, poetic writing; but it has been exceptional, and, until lately, rather much neglected. It is obviously not quite fair to pick Leo Kirschbaum of *Commentary* as the sole exemplar of the well-intentioned, easygoing readerhood, for he has tried not to be careless or casual, and has indeed worked hard at his assignment. But in him the moral becomes beautifully clear: as a sharp reader of Elizabethan tragedy, and as one who understands poetic values, he is precisely the person who ought to read *All the King's Men* with especial discernment. Yet his trouble is that, as a man of the long post-1700 age of prose, he somehow approaches the novel with a totally different set of assumptions—an approach which is tantamount to an abdication of his critical powers. As a modern work, the novel is going to be explicit, straightforward, resonantly in favor of the accepted goods, adapted to intelligent upper-middle-class sentiments, not too poetic, and with the philosophy, if any, prompting pretty audibly from the wings; and if the work draws its skeletal materials from modern history, it must stick faithfully to what we all know to be the truth about those materials. Now Dr. Kirschbaum would never read Shakespeare or Sophocles like that. He would unconsciously junk all these preconceptions and start with the text. But in his modern *acedia*—and perhaps it is the literary *acedia* of any age—he starts, alas without knowing it, with something else that the text is supposed to fit into. So he misses entirely the central theme—the split in modern consciousness; in Jack's unrelenting philosophical inquiry he finds only callow, even pathological insufficiency; and the complex attitude of Jack to Willie, which involves not only his being hypnotized by the genius of action, but also his sense of guilt and his paradoxical detachment and critical distance from Willie, Kirschbaum takes to be an "amoral and mystical approval of the American fascist Willie Stark."

It may be worth repeating, as we leave the reviewers, that enough of them glimpse the novelist's intention to establish his power of communication. Those who miss it are, in the main, not at all dull; but by some habit of thought, some cast of mind, which seems to come from the mental sets of the civilization, they are blocked off from seeing how the novel, as tragedy, works. Mr. Warren treats them as independent minds, able to slip away from societal apron strings. In fact, he never condescends to his readers: those who would read him aright will have to work out careful patterns. It would have been easy to supply a chorus identifying Willie's half-truths as half-truths; but Warren does it indirectly by having Willie in effect repudiate—his attitude to the hospital denies his formal relativism—his own announced positions, and by having the implicit repudiation seen through the awareness of a Jack Burden who is himself experimenting with concepts. Jack could have underlined his reservations about Willie, but we only see those reservations nibbling at the edges of an apparently whole-souled commitment. In the midst of strenuous muckraking Jack tells Willie, "I'm not one of your scum, and I'm still grinning when I please," and thus we see both the split in Jack and the withheld area of self which differentiates him from the Duffys and Larsons. The split in Jack—that is, the split in an age—finds a symbol in half-truths, with which the difficulty is precisely that they are partly true. While striving toward a whole, Jack veers from half to half. In early years he is inactive, his personality is diffuse and amorphous. There is no imperative in either tradition or work; as a lover he ends—this is one of the most delicately managed episodes—in a hesitation which is in origin an echo of an old honor, thinned out now into a wavering sentiment, and which is in effect a negation. What Anne does not find in Jack she finds in Willie; what Jack does not find in himself he finds in Willie—resolution. But, riding on another man's activeness, Jack the doer is never free of Jack the self-critic; he justifies by half-truths, but: he also accepts half-truths uttered in judgment. The photographer says, "...you work for Stark and you call somebody a son-of-a-bitch." He is half right, half wrong, Jack thinks, "and in the end that is what paralyzes you." Now the sense of paralysis is ironically a symbol of reorientation: Jack is trying to make his action and his idea cohere—a private parallel to his outward act of bringing Adam and Willie together. But the still more embracing irony, the irony which is all the preachment for which anybody could wish lies in Willie's relation to his half-truth world. For his dubiety of his official philosophy is activated too late. For him the half-truth of acting according to the facts has been a whole truth; of the paralysis of others he is born; from the start he is always shown acting; and in turn all the spirit, the essence of action has somehow formed young Tom Stark. What is the end of Tom Stark? In the hospital bed he lies *paralyzed*—a fine climax to the counterpoint of kinesis and paralysis and a symbol of Willie's real failure. Willie, as Jack says, "could not tell his greatness from ungreatness and so mixed them together that what was adulterated was lost."

Who would read the book aright, we have said, must find the patterns. Jack, searching for a past, kills his father; Willie, searching for a future, may be said to kill his son. What Willie learns, there is not enough life left to define wholly; it is Lucy who seizes, in a quiet irony, the instrument of continuity into the future. Jack finds a truth, a basis for values, a faith. All this is part of a very complex theme of past-and-future, a theme which is really another way of presenting the split in the world. Here the split is defined chronologically; the separation of fact and idea is also man's separation from his roots, a separation which appeared extensively in *At Heaven's Gate* and which appears intensively here. Jack's separation from the past is so extreme that at first he cannot understand Cass Mastern's acute sense of moral responsibility; the essence of his inner development in his coming to terms with the past, knowing the reality of guilt, and learning, with Cass, that "the world is all of one piece." There is a skillfully managed irony in the ambivalence of the past: when it is no longer a nourishing tradition, it is a terrifying skeleton: *the* past is gone, and each man has only *a* past that he can be coerced with. The skeleton, the sterilizing past, is all that Willie professes to believe in (even while being drawn to the Burdens, who represent traditions, the fertilizing past): Jack digs up each man's past and discovers *the* past; from case histories he progresses to the meaning of history. He moves away from his old misvaluation of the past, of which the two faces are cynicism and sentimentality. "...we can keep the past only by having the future, for they are forever tied together." "...only out of the past can you make the future." Faith is proved by deed, and fruitful deed comes only out of the long wisdom. He is, at last, prepared to face history, to enter "the awful responsibility of Time."

Shift a few pieces on the board, and the history theme becomes the knowledge theme, which can be traced from episode to episode and from reflection to reflection. "Life is Motion toward Knowledge," Jack argues. Willie's career is a progression in self-knowledge, and Jack's is a passion for knowledge that leads from factual to moral awareness. "...all knowledge that is worth anything is maybe paid for by blood." Jack's self-criticism is important here—the innumerable passages in which he catches himself at lying, or self-deception, or histrionics; or understands his feeling that Duffy "had... like a brother winked at me...." Or shift a few pieces again, and the action theme becomes a study of participation and withdrawal, with its echoes in Jack and Adam and Hugh Miller, and the conclusion to which it leads, that there are no perfect choices: "...there is always a price to make a choice." In one sense the body of the work is the regeneration theme: the variations range from a prefrontal-lobotomy to the Scholarly Attorney's efforts with "unfortunates" to the acquisition of new insights by Cass Mastern and Jack Burden.

As the consciousness of an age, Jack also embodies its philosophic searchings. Jack appears first as an idealist, and there is a nice implied contrast between his version of Platonism, which rationalizes away responsibility, and Adam's, which takes insufficient account of the facts. Then Jack plunges into pragmatism, but it is a drug and never a very efficient one; under the pressure of pain he falls into mechanism—the Twitch theory. But eventually he rejects the world as idea, the world as act, and the world as mechanism; these are the half-truths of a disintegrating order. What he envisages is a saving union of the idealist and pragmatist impulses of modern man; while the brilliance of Willie is his executive mastery of fact, his greatness, in which the others "must" believe—the margin between him and the ordinary political operator—is his emergent awareness of the inadequacy of fact. If they cannot believe in that, there is nothing left; but they can believe, for tragedy reaffirms the whole truth which measures the failure of the incomplete man. Humpty is Willie and he is also Jack— that is, the man who has broken into parts. Nor will men and horses, human intention and mere animal strength, reunify man. That is, reintegration transcends the secular; Jack moves, at the end, toward the deepest possible grounding of his world view, a grounding in theological terms. He assents, "in his own way," quasicommittally, to a metaphysic which accommodates evil, not to despair, but to define salvation. The reader recalls the earlier words of the Scholarly Attorney, "God is Fullness of Being." Humpty is partialness. The fall in the old rhyme becomes a version of his Fall.

Some such matters the critics may reasonably be expected to see. Let it be said, if it need be said, that no one expects them to see more than the evidence. They need not like the evidence—a situation which as we all know, *non est disputandum;* they need not consider the evidence sufficient to prove what the author wants proved. For various reasons they may not like the author's looks. If they think him unhandsome, that's their privilege; but, it may be repeated, they are wholly obliged to take a good, long, direct look at him instead of using one of those hasty city-street snapshots at twenty-five cents a peep. What contests he will win will appear in time. But those who have looked close enough to realize the intellectual and imaginative richness will know that they have been at least in the neighborhood of greatness. There is room, perhaps, for further coalescence of the gifts that appear brilliantly in, for instance, the vitality of Willie, the ironic commentary of Jack, the Jack-Anne idyl and the weak spot where it is breached, the bursting fullness ge, the reflective probing. For the present reader there is still, for some reproportioning and for some filling out, with the logic of feeling and motive and the immediate concretenesses of man in action, of the immensely moving symbolic paradigms whose rightness carries one into wholeness of admiration and into all but wholeness of assent.

The Narrator's Mind as Symbol:
An Analysis of
All the King's Men

by Norton R. Girault

If we are to judge from many of the reviews, *All the King's Men* is a very difficult novel to "explain"—difficult, it appears, mainly because of the oblique first-person narrator point of view. There have been many comments about the irrelevance of Jack Burden, as if he were a sort of displaced person who had found his way into the novel through the servants' entrance, or an exhibit guide with an annoying habit of stopping in the middle of his discourse upon the exhibit to digress on his domestic problems. Actually the novel is a dramatic monologue on a grand scale, and Jack Burden is as much the protagonist as he is the commentator. But it is apparent that the story has not been read as a product of Jack's mind. Attempts to explain Willie Stark, for example, have often dodged the problem of taking Jack's statements in character; apparently it has been assumed that the reader sees Willie Stark at first hand and not through Jack's sensibility, and that Willie can be understood and interpreted whether Jack is or not. Such an assumption is enough to cause serious misreading, because out of the first-person narrator point of view grows an important aspect of the novel's theme—that an understanding of the world depends upon an understanding of the self: Jack Burden cannot understand Willie Stark until Jack understands himself. (There is a question, of course, as to whether Jack ever fully understands either himself or Willie Stark.) We can get at an understanding of Robert Penn Warren's interpretation of the Boss only through a perception of the way in which the Boss's story was experienced by Warren's first-person narrator.

"The Narrator's Mind as Symbol: An Analysis of *All the King's Men*" by Norton R. Girault. From *Accent,* 7, 220-34. Reprinted by permission of the author and the publisher.

I

Jack's story is so intimately related to Willie's that, as the narrative develops, their stories are told simultaneously. But phrases along the way like "at least that was the way I argued the case back then" remind the reader of the fact that Jack has lived through the actions he is describing and that he is trying to reorient himself in relation to them. It becomes more and more apparent as the story develops that Jack is telling it as a means of defining to himself what actually did happen to him: the manner in which he reconstructs the story gives the reader an insight into the nature of Jack's experience. For example, the fact that Jack withholds his father's identity until he learns that Judge Irwin has killed himself implies that he wants the discovery of the truth about his paternity to make the same shocking impact upon the reader that it made upon him; it is his way of dramatizing his reaction to the discovery. And when he attempts to describe subjective reactions to events that are past, the metaphors he uses provide the reader with an insight into why Jack Burden is an appropriate first-person narrator. A study of those metaphors indicates that they support a basic symbolism of rebirth that runs through the novel and unifies it, and after our participation in the total experience of *All the King's Men*, we realize that it is because Jack has been reborn, though not of woman (in a sense defined by the symbolism), that he is qualified to tell us what happened to Willie Stark.

The symbolic event that brings the rebirth symbolism into focus is Jack's being awakened in the middle of the night by his mother's screams. It is a "bright, beautiful, silvery soprano scream" that awakens him, and his mother, hysterical, accuses him of having killed his father. The accusation comes as the sudden revelation of the truth about his paternity: Judge Irwin, not the Scholarly Attorney, suddenly becomes his father. Jack has, as his mother charges, killed his father (his attempt to blackmail the judge for the Boss results in the judge's suicide); but he has also created a father, for it requires the violence of the suicide to wring from his mother, out of her love for Judge Irwin, the long suppressed information which gives Jack self-definition. The scream signalizes Jack's rebirth (symbolically, it is a scream of labor pain) in that it gives him a new mother and a new father, both of whom he can accept. It disintegrates his conception of his mother as a woman motivated by vanity and cupidity ("for years I had condemned her as a woman without heart"), because it reveals to him his mother's capacity for love; and it disintegrates his conception of his father as the weak, pious Scholarly Attorney, for in Judge Irwin Jack gains a father he can accept. The scream seems to release something in him, to allow him to see the world for the first time. It allows him to understand Willie Stark, but why it does Jack cannot say. He simply knows that his knowledge of the Boss and of himself grew, finally, out of the scream, that it marked the climax of his story.

Jack's story builds toward his mother's scream in terms of his struggle to resist rebirth. At the beginning of the novel, he sees the Boss's eyes bulge as he begins a political speech and feels the "clammy, sad little foetus" which is himself, huddled away up inside himself, cringing away from "the cold hand in the cold rubber glove" reaching down to pull him out into the cold. Jack feels that he is on the brink of a discovery about the Boss, but subconsciously he seeks the coziness of "not-knowing." His hesitation in his love affair with Anne Stanton results, in part, from the same sort of recoil from knowledge. And his dive and underwater embrace with her are an attempt to submerge himself along with Anne in a cozy womb-state of "not knowing." (The medium will not retain them, of course, and they burst forth into their separateness.) Finally, this subconscious shrinking from a particular kind of knowledge becomes on Jack's part an attempt to repudiate his sensibility, an attempt begun as a result of his frustration in his love affair with Anne and of his dissatisfaction with his past (as symbolized by his parents). On the verge of the sexual act with Anne, he had sensed that to "know" Anne he would have to violate his image of her; he hesitates long enough to disrupt their love affair.

What Jack is searching for is a womb-state of innocence in nature in which his image of Anne will be preserved. And this search becomes a dominant motif leading up to his expulsion from the womb when he unwittingly causes the death of his father. Just before his discovery that Anne has become the Boss's mistress, he sits in his office and envies the jaybird perched in the tree outside his window:

> I could look down and think of myself inside that hollow chamber, in the aqueous green light, inside the great globe of the tree, and not even a jaybird there with me now, for he had gone, and no chance of seeing anything beyond the green leaves, they were so thick, and no sound except, way off, the faint mumble of traffic, like the ocean chewing its gums. (p. 281)*

*[Page references are to The Modern Library Edition of *All the King's Men*, 1953 — Ed.]

The associations with Jack's underwater dive with Anne are significant. Then, when this reverie is interrupted by his discovery of Anne's "infidelity" (of the Boss's violation of the image), Jack flies to California in an attempt to "drown himself in the West." In all these struggles to lose himself in nature, there is a paradoxical struggle toward rebirth: the greater the struggle to resist rebirth, the greater the counter-struggle toward rebirth, as if Jack's nature, unformed, were enveloped by the womb of total nature, which reacts convulsively to reject him. Through his attempts to lose himself in nature, Jack is actually struggling, without realizing it, toward a discovery of his separateness in nature.

The significance of Jack's struggle to resist rebirth may be stated in these terms: Jack shrinks from the discovery of evil, of the taint in nature, of imperfection in the scheme of things. He has seen ugliness and imperfection and, with a cynical smugness, acknowledges their presence in nature, but he does not want to discover evil in himself. Subconsciously, he shrinks from the terrible knowledge that he is capable of good and evil, but until he is reborn through a revelation of the guilt he shares with humanity, he is not fully man, but rather embryonic and amoral. This aspect of the symbol's meaning is pointed up by a conversation Jack has with Lucy Stark about her son Tom's alleged fatherhood of an unborn child (it is significant in terms of the novel's structure that this conversation occurs just before Jack's rebirth):

> "It's just a baby," she almost whispered. "It's just a little baby. It's just a little baby in the dark. It's not even born yet, and it doesn't know what's happened. About money and politics and somebody wanting to be senator. It doesn't know about anything—about how it came to be—about what that girl did—or why—or why the father—why he—"
> She stopped, and the large brown eyes kept looking at me with appeal and what might have been accusation. Then she said, "Oh, Jack, it's a little baby, and nothing's its fault."
> I almost burst out that it wasn't my fault, either, but I didn't.

(356)

The irony, once the symbolism is understood, is obvious. The state of innocence Lucy has described is what Jack has been trying to discover in his attempts to drown himself in nature. He has been trying to hide in the dark where nothing will be his fault.

Fourteen pages later (about a week has passed), Jack is awakened by his mother's scream, and is shocked into the revelation that it has been his fault that his father has committed suicide. "At the moment,"

Jack says, "the finding out simply numbed me." On a literal level, he is referring to his discovery that Judge Irwin is his father. But, symbolically, what numbs him is the disintegration of his whole conception of himself. He has been sick with "the terrible division" of his age. His sensibility dissociated by his repeated attempts to escape into a womb-state of innocence, he has been living in a world out of time and divorced from experience, a world in which his actions have been neither good nor evil, but meaningless. Then suddenly, in one shocking experience, this illusory world is shattered, and he cannot define himself in relation to the new world (in which Judge Irwin is his father and a woman capable of love is his mother). When Jack's revelation of the truth about his paternity is taken along with all the examples in the novel of attempts to change various characters' conceptions of the world, it can be seen that his revelation is a commentary upon these other attempts to cure modern man of the sickness of his age. Jack himself, as the Boss's private detective, has tried to change other men's pictures of the world. He has tried to change Adam's by giving him "a history lesson"; and, ironically, he has caused his father's death by trying to change Judge Irwin's convictions about Willie Stark. Finally, in Adam Stanton's operation on the brain of the man suffering from catatonic schizophrenia, we have the attempt through surgery to change the picture of the world man carries around in his head; after the operation, Jack tells Adam, "Well, you forgot to baptize him—for he is born again and not of woman," and, ironically, baptizes the patient in the name of the Great Twitch, symbol of one of Jack's attempts to submerge himself in nature. (Again, it is significant that this operation occurs before Jack's rebirth; Jack's wisecrack foreshadows the event and he does not realize the symbolic meaning it supports.) In one sense then, the whole novel depicts men "incomplete with the terrible division of their age," suffering from a schizophrenia they do not understand, men whose hope lies not in change from without (through surgery, "history lessons," and the like), but from rebirth from within. And because of the nature of Jack's malady, it is plausible that it should take some time for him to formulate a definition of what has happened to him.

The beginning of his reorientation is his discovery that he is, as his mother charges, guilty of his father's death. He realizes that by killing his father he has created him, and gradually he becomes aware of the fact that all of his detective work for the Boss has been a search for a father to replace the weak, pious fool he believed the

Scholarly Attorney to be. The subconscious motive for his becoming
the Boss's private detective is his attempt to find a father in Willie
Stark, and his fidelity to the Boss is symbolic of his having sub-
stituted him for the alleged father with whom he is dissatisfied. But
when, in Judge Irwin, Jack gains a father he can accept, he no longer
requires the Willie Stark father-symbol; symbolically, the very
detective work he has been hired by the Boss to do results in the end
in the Boss's own death. In chapter nine, the day after the Judge's
funeral, Jack walks into the Boss's office and refuses to do any more
detective work for him. He wonders why, in fact, he does not quit
the Boss's organization altogether. And, thinking of the Scholarly
Attorney and Judge Irwin, he says, "True, since I had lost both
fathers, I felt as though I could float effortlessly away like a balloon
when the last cord is cut." But Jack has lost not two but three fathers
—the Scholarly Attorney, the judge, and, though he does not realize
it, the Boss—so, still numb from the disintegration of the conception
of his father, he is unable to quit the Boss's machine.

Jack remains to discover, after the Boss's assassination, that it is he
himself who has set the events in motion which culminate in the
Boss's own death. After the Boss has died, Jack's independent detective work uncovers the complicity of Sadie Burke and Tiny
Duffy (they are as responsible as Adam Stanton for the Boss's
murder), but Jack discovers his own complicity too, for he sees that
it is his earlier detective work that has produced the facts which led
to the involvement of Anne and Adam Stanton in Willie Stark's
enterprises and which made Sadie's revenge and Duffy's opportunism
possible. But, ironically, the Boss has hired Jack to produce these
facts. The Boss has engineered his own assassination. Guilt for the
slaying seems to spread throughout the novel among all the characters. What shocks Jack is the discovery that his crime (as opposed
to those of Sadie Burke, Tiny Duffy and Adam Stanton) is that his
actions have been meaningless; the others have intended to kill the
Boss, whereas he has intended to be the hired research man in search
of objective fact, as faultless and amoral as Sibyl Frey's unborn baby.
This perception of his spiritual sterility occurs when Jack is unable
to go through with "the perfect duplication of what Duffy had done"
(that is, effect the murder of Duffy by putting the idea in Sugar-
Boy's head); Jack sees that he is as guilty as Duffy, that his murder
of Duffy would, ironically enough, be as meaningless as Jack's
unintended murder of the Boss. Jack is appalled by this discovery
that he has been "caught in a monstrous conspiracy":

> I hated everything and everybody and myself and Tiny
> Willie Stark and Adam Stanton...They all looked alike
> And I looked like them.   (442)

But what saves Jack from this loathing for himself and the world
is another discovery that grows out of his rebirth—the discovery of
his capacity for love. When he learns that his mother is leaving the
Young Executive, the scream is brought back to him in such a way
that he is able to formulate a partial definition of its meaning; it
releases him from his disgust with the world:

> The first hint was in the wild, silvery scream which filled the house
> when the word of Judge Irwin's death was received. That scream rang
> in my ears for many months, but it had faded away, lost in the past and
> the corruption of the past, by the time she called me back to Burden's
> Landing to tell me that she was going to go away. Then I knew that
> she was telling the truth. And I felt at peace with her and with myself.
> (458)

His mother's leaving (in that it is evidence of her love for Judge
Irwin) makes him capable of loving her, and of loving the world
(as his marriage to Anne indicates).

Jack Burden's reorientation grows out of a combination of events
that begin with Judge Irwin's death. And after he has seen his friends
die and his mother leave the Young Executive, he can see a justice in
the injustice of a nature that man can never fully know. Like Cass
Mastern, Jack has discovered that man cannot escape guilt, and he has
discovered too that it is only through an acceptance of the evil in his
nature that man can achieve good. He can even say that in his "own
way" he is not certain that he does not believe the theological
harangues of the Scholarly Attorney (symbol, perhaps, of the Christian tradition in the modern world). Through his rebirth, Jack has
caught sight of the limits, and likewise the potentialities, of human
knowledge. He had lived a long time in terms of a false conception
of his paternity, and, through killing his father, had discovered his
ignorance. He learns that man can never be sure of his knowledge:
one can never fully know one's father. (There can be a pun in Warren's father-symbolism that equates man's knowledge of his temporal
father with his knowledge of the Heavenly Father.) The only knowledge that Jack can be sure of is that tragic waste grows out of the
limitations of human knowledge; therefore, man must strive constantly for that state *least* wasteful of human good. And so, as the
novel ends, Jack Burden speaks of going into the "convulsion of the

world" (the everchanging nature wherein he may be saved from the illusion of the absolute power of human knowledge) "and the awful responsibility of Time" (man's moral responsibility for the illusion of nature he creates).

II

Jack is qualified to tell Willie Stark's story because it, too, is a story of rebirth, and, although Jack does not call it that in so many words, the terms he uses to describe it are significant. Huddled over his law books, Willie is "in a room, a world, inside himself where something was swelling and growing painfully and dully and imperceptibly like a great potato in a dark, damp cellar," and "inside him something would be big and coiling and slow and clotting till he would hold his breath and the blood would beat in his head with a hollow sound as though his head were a cave as big as the dark outside. He wouldn't have any name for what was big inside him. Maybe there wasn't any name." And, like the knowledge Jack gains through rebirth, the Boss's knowledge comes to him with the shock of revelation. When Willie realizes (before he has become the Boss) that the Harrison machine is using his naive political idealism to exploit the voters, it is—as Jack puts it—as if Willie had been on the road to Damascus and had seen a great light. When he says this of Willie at the time of Willie's great disillusionment, Jack is not aware of how apt his allusion is, and even after the years that separate his telling of the story from the event, he is not certain what name he should give Willie's "blind, inner compulsion" ("Maybe there wasn't any name."), but through his own rebirth, Jack gains an insight into the meaning of the Boss's life.

The Boss's story starts with a revelation and ends with a revelation. At the beginning of his story, it is revealed to him (through his "luck") that man must run counter to amoral nature and that man must create human good out of human bad. (Willie learns this when the crooked politicians in the state try to "run it over him like he was dirt.") But when Willie tries to spread the light among his countrymen, when he tries to awaken them to an awareness of their responsibility as human beings to separate themselves from exploitable nature, he is frustrated by their failure to understand. They roar their applause, but they do not see, actually, what is behind the bulging eyes and the forelock of hair. They are as ready for Willie to run it over them like they were dirt as they were to be exploited by the Harrison outfit. Nevertheless, the Boss's conviction, gained through a sort of revelation, impels him to persist stubbornly throughout the novel in his attempt to achieve a political state based on the assumption that men are all, potentially at least, like himself—capable of seeing the light. He becomes "the cold hand in the cold rubber glove" trying to wrest men from their submergence in brute nature. But in trying to enforce on them from without a knowledge he gained from within himself, the Boss is trying to usurp the work of the mysterious principle which brought him his knowledge. It is the same principle which operates through Jack Burden to cause his rebirth and, finally, through the Boss to kill him. But in the death of the Boss the knowledge he has tried to live by is reaffirmed; Willie realizes that what has killed him is his own failure to believe in the knowledge of his earlier revelation. So the Boss's story ends with a revelation ("It could have all happened different, Jack"), and the Boss is reborn in the sense that he regains, on his death-bed, a conviction in the validity of the knowledge which has made him the Boss.

Whereas Jack Burden's story starts out with his attempts to submerge himself in nature, the Boss's story begins with his attempt to separate himself from nature. It is as if he were trying to prove, by exploiting it as it had never been exploited before, that the human in nature will finally react to resist exploitation and prove itself capable of self-realization, just as Willie had reacted when they tried to run it over him like he was dirt. Throughout his career we have Nature standing in animal-and-plant-dumb commentary upon the Boss's actions: the stoic cows standing in the mist along the highway staring dumbly at the soaring Cadillac, the 'possum and the moccasin trying to cross the Boss's path only to be run down and churned thumpingly to death against the underside of the fender. And the domestic animals are absorbed into the symbolism: the family dog Buck in the first chapter, whose uncooperative carcass is a latent hint of the recalcitrancy of the unpredictable, uncontrollable, natural factor not only in animal but in human nature as well (Buck is equated with Old Man Stark in terms of the politically exploitable in Willie's past). Also, in many of the images, there is an equating of Willie's constituency with brute nature: "the gangs of people who looked at me with the countryman's slow, full, curious lack of shame, and didn't make room for me to pass until I was charging them down, the way a cow won't get out of your way until your radiator damn near bats her in the underslung slats." This is the nature in which Willie Stark seeks affirmation of the knowledge that isolates him.

Willie's apparently brutal and vindictive treatment of Byram B. White, erring State Auditor, reflects the Boss's grinding, probing attempt to prove to himself that man can detach himself from brute nature. It is more than a simply graphic metaphor that we get in Warren's description of Byram's bodily reaction to the Boss's verbal abuse: Byram draws himself "into a hunch as though he wanted to assume the prenatal position and be little and warm and safe in the dark." The Boss is trying to force Byram's rebirth. And when Byram has left, the Boss tells Jack:

> I gave him every chance...Every chance. He didn't have to say what I told him to say. He didn't have to listen to me. He could have just walked out the door and kept on walking. He could have just put a date on that resignation and handed it to me. He could have done a dozen things. But did he? Hell, no. Not Byram, and he just stands there and his eyes blink right quick like a dog's do when he leans up against your leg before you hit him, and, by God, you have the feeling if you don't do it you won't be doing God's will.   (142)

The same impulse that makes him vilify Byram in an attempt to make the man separate himself from nature drives the Boss to try to talk Adam Stanton into a realization that he can never detach himself from nature in an absolute sense. Adam and Byram represent opposite extremes of modern man's condition; they symbolize attitudes the Boss's revelation has shown him to be false.

Ironically, what makes the Boss's political success possible is the fact that his countrymen create in him a hero, an alter ego, and the Boss is unable to get through that alter ego to them. He wants to show them the light he has seen, to prove his knowledge (to himself as well as to them) by changing the picture of the world they carry around in their heads. But his downfall is a result, finally, of his inability to break down the false conceptions of him held by the various members of his machine and by his constituency, by his failure, in other words, to make them understand the principle on which his actions are based. One of the greatest ironies of the book is that the Boss thinks that among all his men Jack Burden alone really understands him. When the others have left them alone, the Boss confides in Jack as if Jack will understand where others have not. But in one sense Jack is simply a more complicated and highly developed version of Byram B. White and of the people who make up the Boss's constituency, who want "the nice warm glow of complacency, the picture that flattered him and his own fat or thin wife standing in front of the henhouse."

Willie is a symbol of man's struggle toward integration in terms of his whole nature. This integration is symbolized by the successful control and cooperation he maintains in his political machine. All the Boss's men working in harmony symbolize an integration of a sort within the Boss. Separately, each is a symbolic correlative for an aspect of the Boss's nature. When the Boss begins to try to operate independently of any one of them, the integration begins to crumble. When he tries to build his hospital without the cooperation of Tiny Duffy, he is trying to insist upon the idealistic aspect of his nature at the expense of the animal—gross and predatory—in his nature. And Tiny Duffy, symbol of this aspect of the Boss's make-up, and Sadie Burke, symbol of the indivisible bond between brute and human nature, participate with Adam Stanton, symbol of the exclusively idealistic in the Boss's nature, to kill him. By allowing these aspects of his nature to get out of hand, to function as isolated impulses, the Boss kills himself. Yet in his death there is a form of salvation, for through disintegration of his personality he is reborn to a realization that man cannot violate the essential complexity of his nature with impunity.

But what Sadie and Adam are trying to kill is an image of the Boss each has created in terms of his own ego—the Boss's integration has been doomed to fall because it has rested on an unsound base. Although the Boss's own choices are responsible for his fall, his incapability of maintaining his integration in the world is a commentary on "the terrible division" of his age. After his death "all the king's men" cannot put him together again; without the principle upon which the Boss's control was based, they do not add up to the microcosm maintained by the Boss's integration. An understanding of the way in which the Boss's men stand as correlatives for aspects of his nature is a key to his characterization.

Sadie and Sugar-Boy are symbols of adjustment to nature in terms of an abstract code. When Sadie informs him of the fraud perpetrated on him by the Harrison outfit, she "made him what he is" (she is the mother of his rebirth), and it is significant that she has developed a sort of honor-among-thieves code of retaliation based on her reaction to her pock-marked face and her besotted father. And Sugar-Boy's relation to nature has been the result of his limitations, too. His stuttering and his puniness at school made the big boys try to "run it over him like he was dirt." So he has developed a code which gives him mastery over his deformity and over other men. Sugar-Boy stands for a kind of counter-predatoriness, which is in harmony with the other elements of the Boss's nature as long as it is held in check. After the Boss's death, Sugar-Boy is set adrift, has no usefulness.

If there is an affinity between the Boss and Sugar-Boy, there is no less an affinity between the Boss and another of the men upon whom he heavily depends early in his career—Hugh Miller of the "clean hands, pure heart, and no political past." There is sincere regret in the scene of their parting: "You're leaving me all alone," the Boss tells him, in semi-comic woe, "with all the sons of bitches. Mine and the other fellow's." Hugh Miller is a part of Willie's nature that he never relinquishes, just as Tiny Duffy is a symbol of "that other self of Willie Stark, and all the contempt and insult which Willie Stark was to heap on Tiny Duffy was nothing but what one self of Willie Stark did to another self of Willie Stark because of a blind, inward necessity." Adam Stanton is a symbol of the Hugh Miller aspect of Willie Stark's nature, and Willie's visit to Adam is motivated by his desire to convince himself of the truth of his self-knowledge.

Ironically, Jack Burden stands for what finally frustrates the Boss's attempt to achieve integration of his whole nature; Jack stands for a malignant skepticism that the Boss puts to work to disintegrate the other characters' conceptions of the world, and which ends in disintegrating the Boss's own conception of himself and of the people around him.

The Boss's affair with Anne Stanton symbolizes Willie's attempt to find in nature some means of achieving good through triumph over the gross and brutal in nature (the Tiny Duffy aspect of his nature). Anne's sculptured, stylized beauty, as opposed to Sadie's pock-marked, blemished face, points up the symbolic contrast between the Boss's two mistresses. It is significant that what brings the Boss and Anne together is her plea to him for assistance in her welfare work, symbol on a smaller scale of what Willie is attempting in his hospital project. Anne's disillusionment about her father and Willie's about his ability to control his son's destiny seem to determine the relationship between Anne and the Boss, as if their affair were a natural outcome of their search for a satisfactory attitude toward nature.

Tom Stark, the Boss's son, is a symbol of human incorrigibility; he is a living rebuff to his father's necessity to find proof in nature that somehow man is controllable. He is continually making not only his father, but himself too, vulnerable to exploitation. To save Tom from marriage to Sibyl Frey, Willie agrees to play ball with the opposition. In his attempt to rectify his son's blunders, the Boss is indulging a sort of parental pride that is in conflict with the code by which he is trying to live. With his eye set on the abstract political objective, the Boss is committed to give up certain of his "necessities" as a human being. But something will not allow him to relinquish his parental pride: this something is the assertion of an essential part of his nature.

The hospital scene produced by Tom Stark's injury brings Sadie, Anne and Lucy together and points up symbolic contrasts already established. Sadie, Anne and the Boss have no defense against the agony of raw grief, but Lucy, guided by her faith in human goodness and love, is able to maintain control of herself and assist her husband, unmanned by his suffering, to leave the waiting room. This is not to say that Lucy becomes the prim heroine of the novel. She does not regain her husband in the end, and we last see her clinging to a faith which makes her capable of adopting a child whose paternity is highly questionable on the long chance that it may be Tom Stark's son, and, symbolically, on the longer chance that Willie may be reborn through it. But Lucy does symbolize a faith which pronounces commentary on the Boss's faith in himself, and on Sadie's faith in her eye-for-an-eye code. Lucy's is a faith in a power before which man is helpless; and it enables her to endure the loss of her husband and of her son; ironically, it affirms the same sort of belief in the potentiality of man as that affirmed by the Boss's dying statement.

Sadie, on the other hand, has no defense against her loss of the Boss. She cannot stay away from the hospital while Tom, whom she has never liked, is suffering. Finally, when she realizes that the Boss is going to leave her permanently, she cannot discipline her attitude toward the loss in terms of her code. She kills the Boss, but, after the murder, she is unable to harden herself to the crime; Jack discovers her in a sanatorium in a state of collapse:

> So I continued to sit there for quite a while, holding Sadie's hand in the silence which she seemed to want and looking across her down toward the bayou, which coiled under the moss depending from the line of cypresses on the farther bank, the algae-mottled water heavy with the hint and odor of swamp, jungle and darkness, along the edge of the expanse of clipped lawn.   (436)

We have in the landscape a juxtaposition of the brute natural and uncontrollable and the rational and man-controlled, the elements which have gotten out of hand in Sadie's nature. But this is not to say that Sadie Burke is the villainess of the novel any more than that Lucy Stark is the heroine. Both Lucy and Sadie operate as dynamic symbols to qualify the central theme. Sadie is frustrated because she tries to live in terms of a code inappropriate to her nature. But she gains self-knowledge through her collapse, and in her letter to Jack after her recovery there is the implication that she has achieved a sort of mastery over herself in terms of this self-knowledge.

The Boss's downfall is a result of his losing sight of the relationship between man and nature. Highway 58 is a symbol of what Willie Stark achieves in terms of his knowledge that good must be built out of the bad in man. Crooked politics result in Highway 58. Throughout the novel sections describing the highway are repeated to develop a symbol of the precariousness of this relationship between man's aspirations to idealism and the inescapable, irrational, gross aspect of man's nature, an aspect he shares with the dense, uncontrolled natural world along the highway: the jungle at the edge of the clipped lawn. As long as he realizes that he is cutting across nature (Sugar-Boy realizes this with a vengeance when he swerves dexterously to run down the 'possum), he may maintain his separateness. But the "ectoplasmic fingers of the mist" reach out of the swamp, "threading out from the blackness of the cypresses" to snag them — an eerie foreshadowing of the climactic catastrophe of the novel.

For Willie Stark loses sight of nature's resistance to complete control. When his son is killed, Willie's story comes to a climax. In the face of this blow, Willie loses sight of the inseparability of good and evil; he determines to fight back and force upon nature man's ability to achieve absolute good; so he sets out to build his hospital solely out of the "good" in man (Tiny Duffy and Gummy Larson are to have no hand in it). In spite of Lucy's insistence that the hospital — "those things" — does not matter in the face of their son's death, Willie sees it as a symbol of man's undaunted march toward triumph over disease and accident; through surgery, man will control accidents of the sort which killed his son. He begins by banishing Gummy Larson, the crooked contractor, and Tiny Duffy, whom he had promised an interest in the undertaking. But he is so hypnotized by his determination to impose his will upon the nature which has taken his son that he loses sight of the fact that he is running rough-shod over Tiny and Gummy and Sadie Burke, as his Cadillac has run over 'possum and moccasin; he becomes hypnotized like the driver who, in an image in the opening page of the book, loses control of his car, crashes over the shoulder of the highway into the weeds, and is killed. Gummy, Sadie and Tiny Duffy have all made him what he is, represent essential parts of his make-up. And, finally, Adam Stanton, symbol of idealism divorced from the brute natural, pulls the trigger. Willie has been struggling toward integration in terms of his whole nature, but the integration among his henchmen breaks down when he tries to divorce idealistic aspirations from their basis in his own pride and selfishness. His downfall is a symbol of the disintegration brought about by modern man's attempt to control the external world through will unguided by understanding. But the Boss's downfall is his "luck"; for through his own disintegration he gains faith in the potentiality of integration in man: he learns that something within man destroys him when he ceases to act as man.

III

Warren's point of view requires that all the imagery of the novel grow out of Jack Burden's mind, and, although it is beyond the scope of this paper to try to do more than suggest the psychological motivation for Jack's reveries, something should be said about the way in which the symbolism considered here is produced by Jack's state of mind.

At the time of the telling of the story, Jack is like a man recuperating, learning to walk again, or like a man whose mind has been liberated from the effects of a drug. He is feeling his way back over territory he had thought familiar, re-exploring it in an attempt to master the knowledge brought to him through his rebirth. Earlier, as a man sick with the "terrible division" of his age, he had seen the world through a diseased sensibility. His feeling of betrayal after the disruption of his love affair with Anne had made him turn on his sensibility as if it had betrayed him, for it had brought between them the image of Anne floating in the bay, had seemed to make him incapable of going through with the sexual act. Jack had tried, after this frustration, to develop a protection against further betrayals, had done so by seeking a "realistic" attitude toward the world. Prior to his rebirth, his speech and actions in the presence of others had shown him to be a man subordinating sentiment to the requirements of the political world in which he worked (and in this respect he had felt he was like the Boss), but in moments of inactivity, he had lapsed into reveries that took the form of ambiguous overflows of sentiment: "You see a cow standing in the water upstream near the single leaning willow. And all at once you feel like crying." After his rebirth, as he looks back on those reveries and reconstructs them, Jack can see that they were symptoms of a disease, but he cannot put a name to the sickness; and, as he tells the story in retrospect, he seems to reproduce those reveries with an almost loving and morbid relish. So what we get in the novel in Jack Burden's "style" (which cannot be equated with Warren's style) is a marked alternation between passages of straight, laconic reporting (Jack Burden describing Jack Burden the ex-reporter) and passages lyrical, rhetorical and often sentimentally ironic (Jack Burden trying to reproduce Jack Burden the ex-romanticist). By more than simple juxtaposition this alternation involves a mutual qualification; one Jack Burden qualifies the other and gives us the whole character: a man whose incorrigibly active sensibility is still resisting his attempts to subordinate it to the requirements of his adopted cynical view. In this alternation the conflict (the struggle toward and against rebirth) which is Jack's hope is dramatized. But the tension and conflict produced by this alternation do more than characterize Jack Burden. They bring to focus several meanings and implications that sharpen our perception of the total intention of the novel; these meanings and implications are brought to focus by the quality such passages possess of functioning in a number of ways simultaneously.

For example, passages produced by his unchecked flow of sensibility occur when Jack "relaxes." Lolling in a hammock while the boss paces the yard pondering a political problem, Jack sees the leaves about his head and reflects:

> I lay there and watched the undersides of the oak leaves, dry and grayish and dusty-green, and some of them I saw had rusty-corroded-looking spots on them. Those were the ones which would turn loose their grip on the branch before long—not in any breeze, the fibers just relax, in the middle of the day maybe with the sunshine bright and the air so still it aches like the place where the tooth was on the morning after you've been to the dentist or aches like your heart when you stand on the street corner waiting for the light to change and happen to recollect how things once were and how they might have been yet if what happened had not happened.   (37)

What starts out as an apparently casual, almost languid speculation about the leaves develops into a vague, aching nostalgia. By a process of association Jack arrives at a sardonic *carpe diem* theme from which he is awakened by the crack of Sugar-Boy's automatic from behind the barn where the gunman is practicing fast draws.

We have here a reverie framed by our awareness of the Boss pacing the leaves and Sugar-Boy practicing his skill (both described in terms Jack Burden the self-styled hard-boiled henchman would use: "Well, it was his baby, and he could give it suck" and "It was Sugar-Boy off down in the lot playing with his .38 Special again"). The irony of the juxtaposition grows out of the terms in which Jack describes the three activities. He feels that he shares no responsibility for the Boss's problem: he is simply doing what he is paid to do. So he relaxes in the hammock in a sort of luxury of irresponsibility, allowing his mind to drift in a vague lack of purpose like the leaves he is contemplating; he is, in his withdrawal, trying to submerge himself in the womb of total nature, but his reflections on the leaves lead him to a contemplation of the inevitability of change. The leaves fall, the tooth deteriorates, the traffic light changes, and suddenly Sugar-Boy's automatic cracks the silence. The critical problem is this: How aware is Jack Burden, at the time of his telling of the story, of the irony of this juxtaposition—Boss pacing, Jack brooding, Sugar-Boy practicing? Certainly, at the time the events took place, Jack was unaware of any irony in the fact that while he mused on the futility of human action Sugar-Boy was diligently practicing a highly developed technique of human action. The fact that Jack forgets the leaves, listens for a while to Sugar-Boy's target practice, then dozes off in the hammock is evidence that he missed the irony completely at the time the events occurred. At the time, much later, of his report of what happened, Jack reconstructs the events in a way that suggests that he is still unable to define the irony of the scene. But the reader, through his insight into Jack's subconscious state of mind, can see how the whole sequence has functioned to point up three conflicting attitudes toward nature which produce the basic conflict in the novel.

Again, in his reverie just prior to his revealing the evidence of her father's participation in crooked politics to Anne Stanton, Jack subconsciously struggles with the conflict produced by his sensibility:

> A month from now, in early April, at the time when far away, outside the city, the water hyacinths would be covering every inch of bayou, lagoon, creek, and backwater with a spiritual-mauve to obscene-purple, violent, vulgar, fleshy, solid, throttling mass of bloom over the black water, and the first heart-breaking, misty green, like girl-hood dreams, on the old cypresses would have settled down to be leaf

and not a damned thing else, and the arm-thick, mud-colored, slime-
slick moccasins would heave out of the swamp and try to cross the
highway and your front tire hitting one would give a slight bump and
make a sound like *ker-whush* and a tiny thump when he slapped
heavily up against the underside of the fender, and the insects would
come boiling out of the swamps and day and night the whole air would
vibrate with them with a sound like an electric fan, and if it was night
the owls back in the swamp would be *whoo-ing* and moaning like love
and death and damnation, or one would sail out of the pitch dark
into the rays of your headlights and plunge against the radiator to
explode like a ripped feather bolster, and the fields would be deep in
that rank, hairy or slick, juicy, sticky grass which the cattle gorge on
and never get flesh over their ribs for that grass is in that black soil
and no matter how far down the roots could ever go, if the roots were
God knows how deep, there would never be anything but that black,
grease-clotted soil and no stone down there to put calcium into that
grass—well, a month from now, in early April, when all those things
would be happening beyond the suburbs, the husks of the old houses
in the street where Anne Stanton and I were walking would, if it were
evening, crack and spill out into the stoops and into the street all that
life which was now sealed up within.   (257-58)

We have in such imagery a complex of references to the basic symbolism. In the water hyacinth metaphor, for example, we have the
principle of natural change and rebirth which is uncontrollable
("throttling mass"), miraculous ("spiritual-mauve," the connotations
of the ecclesiastical robe), gross and irrational (the "obscene-
purple" suggests the membrane in which the foetus huddles: "Violent, vulgar, fleshy, solid," the bestiality of lust), and in the face of
which man seems helpless. We have the "obscene-purple" played
off against the "spiritual-mauve" to produce a tension which reflects Jack's conflicting impulse to worship and loathe nature, to
find mingled hope and despair in natural fruition (the "misty
green" of the cypress is a summons to idealism, to hope in an ultimately "good" end toward which natural process tends; but the
"misty green" turned "leaf and not a damned thing else" seems to
turn the hope to despair, like fragile girlhood optimism frustrated in the adult experience of womanhood). The image of the car
running over the moccasin symbolizes man running counter to
brute natural process (the passage of the highway through the dense,
uncontrolled nature is antagonistic to the passage of the moccasin
impelled by the season to cross the road): part of man's nature separates him from brute animal nature. Yet his idealism is rooted in
the mysterious, uncontrollable, gross and irrational process which

determines his environment. The undernourished cows are re-
minders that nature is, if not inimical to man, at least so organized
that it has no regard for his welfare: the lush fruition of the season
produces insects, snakes, owls, hyacinths, but it barely supports the
domestic animal upon which man depends. One could probe the
passage further and discover new connotations which function to
point up the total meaning of the novel. It is enough here to point
out that the passage creates an atmosphere in which the reader's
sensibility is focused on the mystery which furnishes the basis for
the novel's theme.

It is to such passages as those just considered that critics must
return for a proper evaluation of *All the King's Men*. And those
passages must be read as the product of Jack Burden's mind. Warren's choice of his particularly oblique point of view is an index of
his rigorous and thorough-going ontological approach to the mystery
of good and evil. We have in *All the King's Men* the story of how
Willie Stark was assassinated at the peak of his political career, but
what we experience is that story happening inside Jack Burden's
head. The legend of political power is brought to us through a
medium which dramatizes the limits and validity of human knowledge. In fact, one might say that the whole strategy of Warren's
technique thwarts any attempt to find the simplified, clear-cut answer to the question of political power; the form of the novel forces
the reader to take the Willie Stark story as a mystery—a mystery
thoroughly explored in the psychological terms of Jack Burden's
experience.

The Telemachus Theme in
All the King's Men

by Robert C. Slack

I

Nobody was leaning over him to give him chocolate.

(p. 213)*

The Odyssey speaks to every age in the image and idiom of that age. It was characteristic that it should speak to Victorian England through the voice of an aging Ulysses, honored, respected, yet still desirous of pursuing a dream beyond new horizons. It is just as characteristic that our own century should find its spokesman in Telemachus, the dispossessed young man who is searching for a spiritual father and striving to re-establish a lost relationship with his home, his community, and his world. The Telemachus theme, or something very like it, has found a central place in the work of James Joyce, Thomas Wolfe, Eugene O'Neill, T. S. Eliot, and others (specifically, in the characters Stephen Dedalus, Eugene Gant-George Webber, Yank, and the protagonist of *The Waste Land*). It is also one of the principal themes of *All the King's Men*. Jack Burden is a young man seeking roots that will bind him to the modern world. Like Telemachus he has been dispossessed of his natural inheritance. Early in life he was deprived of the security of belonging to an ordered home and family. When he was six, the man he called father simply walked out. Jack was told only that "he didn't love Mother. That's why he went away" (p. 121). There fol-

"The Telemachus Theme in *All the King's Men*" by Robert C. Slack. From *All the King's Men: A Symposium*, edited by A. Fred Sochatoff and others, Carnegie Series in English, no. 3. (Pittsburgh: 1957), Carnegie Institute of Technology, pp. 29-38. Reprinted by permission of the author and the publisher.

*[Page references are to The Modern Library Edition of *All the King's Men*, 1953.—Ed.]

lowed into the home a succession of husbands for his mother, not of fathers for Jack. First was the tottering Tycoon, who soon wheezed his last asthmatic breath; next, the alien and morose Count Covelli, who before long vanished back into his brimstone; and then, finally, the kept Young Executive, Theodore Murrell, only nine years older than Jack. The succession of men in his mother's life seemed to the growing boy like the constant changes of furniture in her living room: each was a kind of temporary fad. Jack grew up believing his mother incapable of true and lasting love. Consequently the need she had of these men could have had no other effect upon him than staining his conception of her and of his home, and poisoning his whole moral atmosphere.

Moreover, in his adolescence Jack spent less and less time actually in the home. After the death of the Tycoon, Jack was shipped off to school in Connecticut. In the summers, when he was not at camp, he did have intervals at home; but these remained alive in his memory chiefly as picnics and tennis games with Adam and Anne Stanton. What might be called his home life developed into a prevailing pattern of comings and goings. Always when he arrived he felt the expectant hope of a fresh start; yet mixed with that hope was the underlying certainty of a developing contention between his mother and him. And always the contention would break out, Jack baffled and angry, his mother cool and soothing but evasive and firmly unchangeable. Finally would come his sudden departure, back to some impersonal room—to the slatternly apartment of graduate school days, or, later, to the hotel room "where nothing was mine and nothing knew my name and nothing had a thing to say to me about anything that had ever happened" (p. 136).

In such circumstances, it is no wonder that Jack has grown up without developing any sense of direction or any particular notion of what he is going to do with his life. There has been no father whose example might furnish him with a point of departure from which he could launch himself into maturity. The operational drives of Jack's personality have been basically centrifugal, outward in all directions away from a central home-situation which contains only bitterness for him. Thus when we find him asserting himself it is in negative ways. He refuses to go to a college of his mother's choice, and he refuses to let her pay for his schooling; he refuses to be one of her kept men. This assertion of self is something; it reflects a kind of stubborn independence in his character. But it is essentially a negative assertion. Like Telemachus before the visit of Athene, Jack is moving in no particular direction.

Jack's lack of direction first causes him serious difficulty when he falls in love with Anne Stanton. She quickly senses this weakness in him. She is dead in earnest when she asks him, "What are you going to do? Do for a living?" (p. 301) At the time, this problem appears to Jack unworthy of discussion, especially since they could more rewardingly be kissing one another in the moonlight. "Going to blow in your ear for a living," he replies. But Anne is not to be turned aside. Her father is Governor Stanton, who was never a drifter. To Anne, Jack lacks the essential masculine quality if all he wants to do is get some job to which he attaches little importance and which will lead him nowhere. Her concern, she explicitly points out to him, is not with his ability to make money or to achieve distinction in the eyes of the world ("I'll live in a shack and eat red beans if you've got to live that way"—p. 302); but she does expect him to have a definite aim in life.

It takes Jack a long time to become aware that he has this defect; and even then he shields himself from too conscious a recognition of it. Just to satisfy Anne with an answer, in an offhand way he decides to go to Law School. But Anne is well aware that there is no conviction behind his decision; and Jack soon realizes, once he has entered Law School, that he hates everything about it. Eventually his lack of direction is responsible for thoroughly alienating Anne. She tells him so, plainly, but he shies away from facing the issue. He senses it as a failure within him, but he follows what by now is becoming a pattern: he runs away from the recognition of a failure. When it is quite clear that Anne will not accept him as he is, Jack attempts to throw a smoke-screen which will hide the real issue, even from himself. He contrives to bust out of Law School in such lurid circumstances that respectable Anne Stanton will be necessarily cut off from him.

It is essentially the same weakness and the same pattern of response to the weakness that explains his experience with the Cass Mastern papers. Jack (like Telemachus) has begun to move toward a fuller awareness of his own position through an interest in the past, particularly in the past of the tradition to which he belongs. This interest is so genuine and sustained that he almost completes the requirements for a Ph.D. in history. But the story of Cass Mastern brings him face to face once more with the individual man's acceptance of purpose in life. Indeed, this story only too painfully exposes Jack's own inadequacy. But he is unwilling to admit the recognition of what he does perceive subconsciously, and once more he pulls down the window-shade in his mind and runs away. He discovers a new method of retreat, a form of extended coma which he calls the Great Sleep. Jack's retreat from what he might have discovered is thorough. So thorough is it that many years later he summarizes the wisdom he had acquired in graduate school in this cynical observation: "If the human race didn't remember anything it would be perfectly happy...that was what I thought I had learned" (p. 44). He didn't want to be faced with the memories of his heritage. History could be upsetting; it had a way of calling him to account.

Since Jack fears to act with purpose, he reacts in typically stubborn fashion by trying again to act *without* purpose—as he had when he decided to go to Law School. This time he contracts the blind marriage with Lois. It ends in the only way it can—with another Great Sleep and the wrench of disengagement.

II

> *Oh father, father!* but he wasn't in the long white room by the sea any more and never would be, for he had walked out of it...
>
> (p. 213)

So far in his disordered existence, Jack Burden is a kind of Telemachus, without a father-image to support him. The procession of his mother's lovers has ousted him, psychologically, and as a result physically, from any real possession of a home. And his inability to develop a sense of direction or adhere to a determined purpose in life has caused him simply to drift on a current of vexation.

The first positive stage in the development of Telemachus comes when he begins to search for his lost father. Though he does not find his father during the journey to sandy Pylos and to Sparta, his education is advanced significantly.

Jack Burden too has need of a father to whom he can attach himself. The first father-image that he had known was the Scholarly Attorney, but Jack long ago rejected him. He was the one who had run away, and by so doing had filled Jack's heart with bitterness. Jack grew up to look upon him as a sniveling weakling who had not been able to give his mother what she wanted ("whatever the hell it was she wanted"—p. 113), and had simply deserted her and his professional life to become a half-crazy (or perhaps a saintly) evangelist and leaflet-writer. Jack despises his weakness. And yet there is a persistent picture from the past which will not vanish:

the picture of this man in the long white room by the sea, with the rain lashing outside but a warm fire dancing on the safe hearth within, leaning over and holding out a bar of chocolate, saying, "Here's what Daddy brought tonight..." (p. 213). This remembered picture can bring a lump to Jack's throat, but he has learned to tense himself against the emotion. To him the Scholarly Attorney is the father lost, and—since he is still alive—the father despised. Jack stands in desperate need of a father, but this one he bitterly rejects.

Jack has been hurt deeply by the progressive stages of his disinheritance, and his reaction time after time has been to turn his back upon the source of hurt. He has been hurt by the Scholarly Attorney's desertion and by his mother's subsequent way of life; so he has rejected his home. He has been hurt by the loss of Anne Stanton; so he has run off to a futile love-bout with Lois. He has come to a near-awareness of what Cass Mastern represents; but the personal implications in this study are so dangerous that he has deserted it. Through these experiences, Jack has built up a resentment against his community and his own social class and its traditions. Therefore whatever search for a father-image he will make will be *outside* his tradition. Actually, within the tradition there have been two men who could have supplied him with a father-image (and in his boyhood they partly did): Judge Irwin and Governor Stanton. But he has rejected that tradition, and therefore seeks his answer outside it.

The pseudo-father to whom Jack is drawn, consequently, is Willie Stark. Jack gives his allegiance to Willie because he sees that Willie possesses a burning inner conviction and a fierce, irresistible power of will in pursuing that conviction. Jack's own scattered purposelessness is drawn together by the force of Willie's personality, like iron filings by a magnet. Willie knows where he is going and how to get there. These are characteristics which Jack Burden notably lacks. In submitting to the leadership of Willie, Jack is finding some guide of action for his own troubled nature.

His allegiance to Willie is curiously two-sided; he is not simply playing the part of a faithful Achates. It is true that, along with Sugar-Boy and Sadie Burke, Jack is one of the most loyal of the king's men. Even before Willie took him on the payroll, he quit the *Chronicle* for Willie's sake. For Willie's sake he endures the lash of Judge Irwin's tongue, and the disapproval of Anne and Adam Stanton as well as that of his mother. For Willie's sake, Jack uses his talents to dip into cesspools. He is the messenger boy who intimidates

Lowdan with the list of names of the men Willie has coerced into dropping the impeachment proceedings; the research job on Judge Irwin is a nasty business from the beginning, but he carries it through. He turns Adam Stanton over to Willie, and Anne too, though he doesn't realize it at the time. Jack is loyal, all right.

But it is no unquestioning loyalty of a simple, faithful servant. Jack has a strong strain of stubborn resistance in him, and not even Willie can rob him of that. He is never one of Willie's "boys," and he is careful to preserve the distinction. Willie realizes the distinction, and he treats Jack always with respect. When Judge Irwin sneers at Jack's being a "body servant," Willie rises and pours Jack a drink out of deference to the young man's self-respect. Willie discusses his personal affairs with Jack as an equal; he asks Jack's opinion about the treatment of Byram White. Jack will draw the line firmly when he cares to. After the suicide of Judge Irwin, he refuses to engage in any more blackmail for Willie, and Willie respects his unspoken reasons. Furthermore, during the whole association Jack carries an inner wall of resistance to what he is engaged in. He knows that he is playing a dirty game; he has adopted a protective shell of wise-cracking cynicism, and when even that won't shield him, he takes refuge in the brass-bound idealist's denial of reality: "What you don't know don't hurt you, for it ain't real... We were something slow happening inside the cold brain of a cow" (pp. 33, 53). If Jackie Burden didn't exist, then of course he couldn't be committing the shameful deeds that he was committing.

So Jack Burden both is and is not a faithful follower of Willie. He accepts Willie as a father-image, and must to the end assure himself that Willie was a great man. But Willie is not the right father-image for him, and in following Willie, Jack finds himself led into deeper and deeper negation. He causes the death of his real father, hands over the friend of his youth, and sets the stage for the betrayal of the woman he loves. His own outlook on the world passes from hurt cynicism to an utter denial of all meaning in life. Jack has followed the wrong guide, and he comes perilously close to being destroyed.

III

It was like the ice breaking up after a long winter.

(p. 376)

Jack finds his true father only through losing him. The silvery scream of his mother, when she hears that Monty Irwin is dead, is the beginning of a process of discovery for him. The completion of the process we never see. With the discovery Jack begins a new life; he is, as it were, born again in Burden's Landing. The knowledge of his father's identity works profound changes in his outlook, and the novel ends with the prospect of his new life stretching richly before him.

Jack welcomes the discovery that Judge Irwin was his real father. At last he can dismiss the blighting fear that the weakness of the Scholarly Attorney is in his veins. Though he is giving up a good, weak father for an evil, strong one, he is satisfied with the swap. Since childhood he has always respected the Judge, has always associated him with manly activities. When Jack was a boy, he and the Judge made and fired catapults and ballistas; under the tutelage of the Judge he learned to hunt; and throughout his youth there were continual proofs that the Judge was a man of remarkable courage. The Judge had been a fine combat officer in the War, and returned with a medal to prove it. He demonstrated his bravery later when he disarmed his would-be assassin on the streets of Burden's Landing. In his old age the Judge still retained the ability to meet danger face to face. It took a bold man to stand up to Willie Stark, but the Judge did not yield an inch. It took an even rarer quality of courage when Jack confronted him with the evidence of his old shame; but the Judge did not whimper and use the knowledge which would have saved his life. He shot himself, bravely and with decent decorum (Jack took a measure of satisfaction in the fact that the Judge made such a neat job of it). So, in spite of the evil in his past—or perhaps partly because of it—he was a figure whom Jack could look upon as a man, a man who acted with courage and decisiveness, and who accepted full responsibility for those actions. This is the father-image that Jack willingly accepts in place of that of the Scholarly Attorney.

No sooner does Jack make the exchange than the clouded world he has been living in begins to clear. It seems as though the consciousness that he is the son of Judge Irwin actually brings to life in his nature an inheritance of his father's characteristics. He begins to act more decisively. First, he makes it clear to Willie that he will no longer dig out blackmail evidence, under any circumstances, even against the most corrupt of Willie's enemies. He is given a nice clean assignment to work on, a tax bill; and though he is still a functionary in Willie's palace guard, he is withdrawn from the corruption that hangs about the central activities of the state government. While waiting for his father's affairs to be settled, Jack withdraws to the sidelines, toying with the notion of taking off entirely into a genteel-rich retirement.

Consequently, in the catastrophic events which follow, Jack is more a witness and recorder than a directly involved participant. He has undergone a slow transition; he is playing a different role. We have been used to looking upon him as a frustrated Hamlet; now we find him better cast as Horatio, the even-hearted friend who can be counted on in disaster. When Tom Stark is hurt, Jack is the one person who stays with Willie and Lucy through the long night at the hospital. Sadie Burke, skulking in the dark corridors, must turn to Jack for information; so must Anne Stanton. Indeed, on the following day Anne calls him again in distress, and he sets out to find the distracted Adam. Also, there is a change in Willie's attitude toward Jack. Up to this point in the story, Jack has looked upon Willie as the man with a compelling sense of direction and has followed along in his train. But now Willie begins to seek Jack's approval for his actions. His deathbed words, "it might—have been different—even yet" (p. 425), are an appeal for Jack's favorable judgment. If Willie had at one time supplied Jack's need for a father-image, that time is now past. After the fall of Willie, Jack continues to serve as the confidant of those who lost most in that fall. Sadie Burke puts her full confession into his hands, to do with what he judges best. Lucy Stark reveals to him the devotion she feels for her supposed grandson, whom she has named in memory of Willie. Sugar-Boy is willing to do murder at Jack's nod. For an instant Jack holds in his hands the lives of Sugar-Boy and Tiny Duffy, but he spares them. And it is with Jack's help that Anne Stanton is restored to an acceptance of life and given a meaningful future.

Jack's new firmness of character arises out of his acceptance of his heritage. In the past he had condemned his mother as a woman "who lived in a strange loveless oscillation between calculation and instinct" (p. 458); and he had rejected her, together with the weak and sniveling image of the Scholarly Attorney. But now at one stroke he is given the image of a strong father and of a loyal and loving mother, and he can and does accept his past. Not that this past is a bright and shining one, by any means; it is full of evil and agony. But it is *meaningful.* Jack can understand its meaning, in terms of human values which have always been valid for him, and he can associate himself with it.

Now he sees more clearly than ever before the lesson that his experiences have been teaching him. There can be no future for any man unless he accepts his past. Without a past a man can have no home, no reference point, no climate of continuity. To live in an ever-enduring present is to rob existence of all possibility of meaning—to serve the Great Twitch and nothing else. Jack's new faith, the doctrine of responsibility, stands in direct opposition to the service of the Great Twitch. He has come to perceive that a man's decision to act or to refrain from action arises out of his conscious will far too often for him to evade responsibility for his deeds. This insight corresponds to that of the tradition which Jack has inherited. His true father, the Judge, accepted full responsibility for his actions; so did Cass Mastern, and so did Governor Stanton. In a very important way, Jack aligns himself with these men and draws his new strength from the conviction he shares with them.

The fullness of Jack's acceptance of his heritage is sketched in only briefly at the conclusion of the novel, but there can be no doubt that it is a complete reversal of his former outlook. He rejects the Great Twitch. He takes up residence in his father's house (temporarily, it is true; but it symbolizes his acceptance of his heritage). He engages himself once more to tell the story of Cass Mastern, which he now realizes is a portrayal of the heritage. He has undertaken the charge of caring for the Scholarly Attorney in his last days. And he has even approached a sympathetic consideration of the Scholarly Attorney's perception of God ("I was not certain but that in my own way I did believe what he had said"—p. 463). It is no surprise to find that the man whom Jack most admires now is Hugh Miller, so reminiscent of the upright Judge. When Hugh goes back into politics, Jack promises to "be along to hold his coat" (p. 462).

Rediscovering and accepting his tradition does not mean stagnation for Jack. He is not going to burrow deep in it and bury himself in its warm folds. On the contrary, at the end of the story he is soon to leave Burden's Landing and to "go into the convulsion of the world, out of history into history and the awful responsibility of Time" (p. 464). But now he will go into the world armed with the inner strength and sureness that as a dispossessed youth he had formerly so needed. This is the heritage his father has left him.

Robert Penn Warren, like so many other twentieth-century writers, has portrayed the wasteland wanderings of a modern Telemachus. But he has also done a rarer thing: he has brought his Telemachus home.

Burden's Complaint: The Disintegrated Personality as Theme and Style in Robert Penn Warren's *All the King's Men*

by Jerome Meckier

It is impossible to ignore Jack Burden's conclusion that *All the King's Men* is about "the terrible division" of an age.[1] Even if one feels that in the final chapter of the novel (10) Burden is often too explicit in sketching his own and the novel's conclusion, one still cannot pass by Jack's theory that Adam Stanton is "the man of idea" and Willie Stark "the man of fact"[2] and that the gap between these two halves of what should be a single drive or person is particularly modern and also, perhaps, specifically Southern. The theory makes both Adam and Willie fragments of an apparently irrestorable Humpty Dumpty. It also crystalizes the major dichotomies within the novel: the past versus the present, or the theme of idealism against practicality, a theme that is represented symbolically by the womb versus the flood.

Unfortunately, any attempt to read Warren's novel in terms of Jack's final theory about Willie and Adam seems to raise Adam to a position of importance that he occupies only intermittently in the actual story. Perhaps this constitutes a weakness in the book since Stanton is seemingly permitted to have a greater thematic importance than the use that is made of him in the plot can justify. Com-

"Burden's Complaint: The Disintegrated Personality as Theme and Style in Robert Penn Warren's *All the King's Men*" by Jerome Meckier. From *Studies in the Novel* 2; no. 1, p. 7-21. Reprinted by permission of the author and the publisher.

[1]Most interpreters of this novel pay some attention to these words but none regard them as the central passage. See the essays in John Lewis Longley, Jr., ed., *Robert Penn Warren: A Collection of Critical Essays* (New York, 1965) and Elizabeth M. Kerr, "Polarity of Themes in *All the King's Men*," *Modern Fiction Studies*, VI (Spring 1960), 28.

[2]Robert Penn Warren, *All the King's Men* (New York: The Modern Library, 1953), p. 462. Future references are to this edition.

pared to Willie and Jack, Adam is a secondary character, but Jack's theory elevates him to Willie's level. In fact, the whole question of focus in the novel remains a perplexing one. Indisputably, *All the King's Men* is meant to be Jack Burden's story, not only because he tells it but also because he resolves it by allegedly emerging in chapter 10 as a kind of bridge or compromise between idea and fact.[3] Nevertheless, Willie Stark is the center of attraction, despite long periods when he is not physically present in the novel, while Adam, as has been said, seems overtaxed thematically. Even the manner of telling the story is occasionally clumsy. Jack Burden must remind his audience that he is reviewing events that have taught him something, but at the same time he must hold back what was learned as long as possible. Although the narrator writes from an achieved conclusion, he must recreate the evolution of that conclusion without allowing it to color too noticeably the stages preceding it. Thus a line in which Jack asserts that a particular theory is only what he thought then (in the past) is sometimes tacked onto a passage to remind one, rather perfunctorily, that behind the Jack who is functioning in the novel's plot is another Jack who is a changed man.

Admittedly, then, there are problems—perhaps due to weaknesses in the novel—that militate against reading the book according to Jack's final theory. However, such a reading opens up areas in Warren's novel heretofore unexplored. What follows is an attempt to trace the theme of division—or what can loosely be called the theme of split-personality—throughout the novel. The terrible division of an age, one finds, is reflected in many of the characters who are virtually two people. It is also reflected in the schizoid tendencies to be found in the theories with which Jack Burden attempts to explain the nature of life. It is found, perhaps most interestingly, in the schizoid style and structure Burden employs to tell his story. Burden's style is one for which Warren has often been criticized[4] but which is really an extension of the book's thematic conflicts.

[3]There are also several statements by Warren that establish Burden as the core of the novel. In an interview reprinted in Longley's book (p. 36), Warren relates how Burden grew in importance from the sentence or two devoted to him in the verse play, *Proud Flesh*, to become the central character of the novel: "It turned out...that what he [Burden] thought about the story was more important than the story itself."

[4]Thus Longley notes that early reviewers of the novel "felt that Mr. Warren should use a plainer, flatter diction." See *Robert Penn Warren* (Austin, Texas, 1969), p. 17. This is a pamphlet in the *Southern Writers Series* edited by Sam H. Henderson and James W. Lee.

I

Jack Burden writes that "As a student of history...[he] could see that Adam Stanton, whom he came to call the man of idea, and Willie Stark, whom he came to call the man of fact, were doomed to destroy each other, just as each was doomed to try to use the other and to yearn toward and try to become the other, because each was incomplete with the terrible division of their age." In attributing a meaning and a philosophy to each man, Jack is not only transforming Willie and Adam into symbolic personages but is also regarding them as projections of a split within himself: a split in which he desires both escape and involvement, in which he cannot fuse his past (in the somewhat aristocratic world of Burden's Landing) with the present (his job in the State House where he works for a redneck governor). Through his inability to connect past and present, Jack's burden becomes synonymous with that of the modern South, a South in which the descendants of Governor Stanton and men like Judge Irwin seem infinitely separated from Willie Stark and the people who support him. These divisions—between Adam and Willie, Burden's Landing and the State House, idea and fact—make the modern age, as it appears in Warren, schizoid and self-destructive, since the two halves of each division are meant to cooperate but can only come into mutually disastrous conflict once the division has taken place.

The extent of the division between Willie Stark and Adam Stanton becomes clearer when Jack defines Adam as an intellectual idealist in full flight from a sordid world. He insists Adam is "a romantic" who believes that "there was a time a long time back when everything was run by high-minded, handsome men" (p. 262). Willie contends, in a somewhat biblical style, that "Man is conceived in sin and born in corruption and he passeth from the stink of the didie to the stench of the shroud" (p. 54); but Adam, says Jack, expects the world to conform to the picture of it he has in his head or else he throws the world away. If there is goodness in the world, Willie insists, one must make it and one must "make it out of badness.... Because there isn't anything else to make it out of" (p. 272). Thus Willie and Adam represent the split in modern life between realism and romanticism, between the world of abstract values (idealism) and the grim, practical world that is allegedly the reality.

Throughout the novel, the world of idea finds its symbol in the womb, and there is, at least initially, a suggestion that the world of idea is one of unpardonable escapism—particularly when opposed by the more commendable arena of responsibility and commitment symbolized by the flood. But it becomes clear that despite the fact that he has turned his back on Burden's Landing to work for a red-neck governor, Jack is as much an escapist as he is a man of fact. Although his position with Stark might seem to show that Jack is satisfactorily oriented towards practical reality, his overly cynical responses to both Adam Stanton and the upright Hugh Miller indicate how much a part of him yearns towards them. Jack is well acquainted with what might be called one's womb-self, with what Jack himself describes as "the dark which is you, inside yourself, like a clammy sad little foetus you carry around inside yourself." In fact, his major mistake in the novel—his reluctance and failure, as a young man, to make love to Anne Stanton—was, as he later realizes, a refusal to "plunge her into the full, dark stream of the world" (p. 328). Thus when Jack brings Adam and Willie temporarily together by persuading Adam to administer the hospital Willie is building, he is attempting to re-fuse the two halves of himself and of the modern age. He is trying to fuse together again the roles of doer and thinker, to give the doer an abstract philosophy to support his actions and the thinker an egress from his womb-like detachment.

But the theme of the modern age as a split personality runs through nearly all of the characters in the book—not just through Adam and Willie—and these characters become a series of rever-berations of the main division in the novel. Every major character is double, that is, has two selves, one of which is frequently as destructive towards the other as, finally, Adam is for Willie. All the king's men, all who come in contact with or work for Governor Stark, seem to be, like Stark himself, in more than one piece and difficult to re-assemble. The novel's structure mirrors this situation as Jack's narrative forsakes chronology and discusses, within any given chapter, several different strands of the plot or relates events from more than one period in Willie's career. The story seems to be in pieces too, just like the characters. On the one hand, there is the upright Judge Irwin who does not scare, in 1936, when Willie threat-ens him and who is one of several father figures for Jack in the novel. On the other hand, there is the Judge Irwin who took a bribe, in 1915, from the American Electric Power Company and in so doing indirectly prompted the suicide of Mortimer L. Littlepaugh. The honest Irwin has forgotten the existence of the bribe-taking Irwin. When Jack resurrects the past, the recollection of the bribe-taker causes the upright Irwin to shoot himself.

The case with Governor Stanton, Adam's father, is similar. Genteel, aristocratic, Stanton represents the golden age of Burden's Landing when neither a governor nor a gentleman would tolerate contact with a Willie Stark. Yet there is a second Stanton who shielded Judge Irwin from exposure at the hands of Littlepaugh, and this Stanton does not differ greatly from the Boss who protects the dishonest State Auditor, Byram B. White. Adam Stanton is, by profession, a surgeon and healer; but, when he assassinates the Boss for having made Anne Stanton his mistress, Adam appears in an opposite role: that of destroyer. Within the romantic idealist, virtually as a separate person, lurks the assassin who commits the act of an anarchist. If Adam is seen as performing here in accord with the dictates of an older, more chivalric South, then in the shooting of Willie Stark one finds the past attempting to destroy a present which it has, in countless ways, but chiefly by negligence and detachment, helped to create.[5]

Schizoid tendencies are not, however, confined to the males in Warren's novel. Sadie Burke also seems to be two people: the Boss' mistress and constant lover despite all his philandering and, indirectly, the Boss' murderess since, through Tiny Duffy, she finally has Willie shot for his infidelity. The whole question of fidelity becomes itself Janus-faced,[6] for by intending to return to his wife, Lucy, Willie is being unfaithful to the same Sadie with whom he was previously unfaithful to his wife. Even Anne Stanton refuses to remain a single person. The romantic image of Anne in Jack's mind, an image of her floating in the water at Burden's Landing, makes her the symbol of frozen, invulnerable youth, of beauty and virginity; but this image is contradicted by the real Anne whose neck, Jack unwillingly notes, is becoming wrinkled with middle age and who has become Willie's mistress (p. 344). Just as it was Jack's unwillingness to violate Anne (or his image of her) that later makes it possible for her to be Stark's mistress, so too the failure of the man of idea—such as Adam or Hugh Miller—to face reality and function in the

---

[5]The extent to which the rise of Stark depends on those who refuse to become involved in modern politics and its issues is made explicitly clear in Robert Penn Warren's *"All the King's Men:* The Matrix of Experience," *Yale Review,* LIII (Winter 1964), 162. Thus Warren is not only anti-totalitarian and anti-fascist, but also, in a healthy sense, anti-traditional and anti-intellectual when either tradition or intellect prevent immersion in life's flood.

[6]The same appears true of knowledge: "The end of man is knowledge, but there is one thing he can't know. He can't know whether knowledge will save him or kill him" (p. 12). One is, however, uncertain here (and elsewhere throughout the book) which of two Jack Burdens is speaking: the Jack who is a participant in the story or the wiser Jack who is looking back as he writes the book.

wòrld of politics and issues made the transformation of Willie the country boy into Willie the Boss inevitable. Jack's failure with Anne is thus on the private level what the failure to participate on the part of Adam Stanton and Burden's Landing is on the public.

Appropriately, Willie Stark is the most collossally split personality in the novel. Even Jack Burden, who knows Willie from 1922 through the late 1930's, feels he is dealing with more than one person. Between Willie the country boy with the Christmas tie and Willie the Boss who breaks men rather than buys them, a sharp and continuous contrast is maintained. The Willie who innocently sips orange pop in Slade's saloon in 1922 may have winked at Jack and thus may even then have contained the later, shrewder Willie. The Boss who dreams idealistically of his hospital seems to recapture at moments the earlier Willie who was Treasurer of Mason County. Despite the change from Cousin Willie to the Boss, Stark is never one to the exclusion of the other. Whenever the Boss makes a speech, Jack contends Willie is transformed and he finds himself wondering which was Willie's true voice, "which one of all the voices?" (p. 12). The extent to which Willie is two people becomes unmistakable when Willie returns home to his father's cabin to take some publicity pictures and his dog fails to recognize in the Boss the Willie he once knew (p. 29).

The split in Willie's personality carries over into the opposing types of imagery associated with him. Jack Burden can never decide whether Willie is Christ or Frankenstein's monster, Abe Lincoln or Machiavelli—for the simple reason, of course, that Willie is all of these. Jack's editor on the *Chronicle* talks of a Willie "who thinks he is Jesus Christ scourging the money-changers out of that shinplaster courthouse" (p. 55); and the Joe Harrison outfit, admittedly with ironic intent, persuades Willie that he is "the savior of the state" (p. 71). What might be called a conversion scene—the barbecue at which Willie, having discovered that he is being used by Harrison, speaks out in his own right—is full of religious terminology as Willie is both the Lamb of God and Paul on the road to Damascus, while Tiny Duffy is Judas Iscariot. Yet one remembers that in Mary Shelley's novel the monster destroys several members of Frankenstein's family. Jack realizes that in writing about Willie in the *Chronicle* he has, in a metaphorical sense, created him, given him an image. And Willie, changed from Jack's portrait of him as "the boy upon the burning deck" into the totalitarian Boss, is responsible, directly or indirectly, for the death of Jack's father (Irwin), for the destruction of Jack's closest friend (Adam), and for the violation of Jack's image of Anne. When he learns Anne has become Willie's mistress, Jack reflects: "somehow by an obscure and necessary logic I had handed her over to him" (p. 329).

Like Abe Lincoln, Willie comes from a log-cabin and studies law. He suffers several defeats, again like Lincoln, before winning a major political victory. His epithet, as was Lincoln's, is the word "honest"—the descriptive adjective he acquires after the collapse of the fire escape at the schoolhouse whose shoddy construction he had tried to prevent. In his first campaign for governor, when he is the dupe of the Harrison outfit, he is accused by Jack of trying to make each of his speeches "a second Gettysburg address" (p. 75). But the split with Lincoln comes after Willie, now governor, survives an attempt to impeach him. Lincoln, Willie recalls, insisted that a house divided against itself could not stand; but, concludes Willie, Lincoln was wrong (p. 165). Willie has divided the legislature against itself and crushed the attempt at impeachment. He has become and remains a modern Machiavelli, an extension of the "cold-faced Florentine" whom Jack pinpoints as "the founding father of our modern world" (p. 417).

After he becomes governor, Willie makes Tiny Duffy—the same man who once helped the Harrison outfit deceive Willie—Highway Commissioner and eventually Lieutenant Governor. Jack explains this by saying that "Tiny Duffy became, in a crazy kind of way, the other self of Willie Stark, and all the contempt and insult which Willie Stark was to heap on Tiny Duffy was nothing but what one self of Willie Stark did to the other self..." (p. 105). Jack implies that Willie knew, perhaps only subconsciously, that he was two people. He implies that in retaining and abusing Duffy, Willie the pragmatist was punishing the innocent and idealistic half of himself that was taken in by Duffy and the Harrison outfit. Burden's explanation makes Willie a schizoid within himself as well as half, in opposition to Adam, of the split that is the modern age. Not only is Willie part of a shattered Humpty Dumpty, of a dichotomy between fact and idea, but he is also, within himself, a Jekyll and Hyde.

All the King's Men is a novel with a realistic plot full of melodramatic excitement, but it also possesses an intriguing symbolic superstructure in which characters and events become representative.[7] Adam and Willie stand for the division of an age, while Jack Burden is the man who, as his name indicates, must bear the burden

---

[7]Thus, as readers of the novel have noted, almost every event in the book has more than a literal meaning. The paralysis of Tom, Willie's son, may thus repre-

of this division.[8] The split between Adam and Willie is one between past and present, between the genteel, somewhat aristocratic South that is represented by Burden's Landing and the rednecks and laborers who support Stark and who are the majority in parts of the modern, democratic South. Jack is involved in both but at home in neither; he cannot accept the past, neither his personal past (his failures with his mother, with Ellis Burden, and with Anne Stanton) nor the more historical past (a world of slavery, chivalry, and, as in Cass Mastern's case, of relentless morality) represented by the doctoral dissertation he began on Cass Mastern's journals but never completed. Uneasy with the past, Jack is scarcely on better terms with the present. His drive westward in chapter 7 and his recurrent need for the Great Sleep are attempts to flee the present and recapture the security of the womb. When Jack ignores the message that begins to emerge from his research on Cass Mastern, he resembles Willie in that he chooses to live and operate purely by means of a pragmatic confrontation with the present. When he retreats from his wife, Lois, or heads West after learning that Anne is Willie's mistress, he becomes Adam; he flees from a reality that fails to match his expectations.

The burden Jack Burden carries is personal and yet, symbolically, it is historical. His refusal to accept the past—at one point he terms the past a "sublunary dung heap" (p. 167)—can be read as the South's failure to face the consequences of its past. The past in this novel is truly a burden for many of the characters: for Jack's mother who must conceal her affair with Irwin, for all the politicians whose past gives Willie a hold over them, and for Jack, the burden of whose past is neatly symbolized by the package that contains Cass Mastern's journals.[9] It accompanies him everywhere he goes. Burden's Landing is aptly named not only because the burdensome past has landed on most of the people from that place but also because the place itself is an encumbrance on the admirable and progressive aspect of Willie as well as the agent responsible, either through withdrawal

---

sent the limitations of pure action, action that, even more so than Willie's, is without any system of values.

[8]Tag names abound in the novel. "Willie Stark," for example, suggests a man of assertive will who is also a stark, disconcerting modern reality. "Adam Stanton" suggests a man who is unfallen, or perhaps cut off from certain kinds of knowledge and experience. The surname implies that Adam, like his father, is to be associated with stability and tradition.

[9]Significantly, Willie, a pragmatist working mainly in the present, has no past that others can exploit but instead uses the past to control others.

from public service or from conservatism while in office, for the creation of conditions that cater to Willie's totalitarian tendencies.

All the King's Men is a historical novel in at least two ways. First, it is about the South of the 1930's, for Stark recalls Huey Long. In fact, it is about the world in that same decade because Stark is the product of drives and forces similar to those that helped Hitler and Mussolini advance. Second, the novel includes a good deal of the South's earlier history. It does this directly in chapter 4 with the story of Cass Mastern, a story in which many of the more shameful factors in the South's past figure as themes. And it does this indirectly or by implication when events in the present seem virtual re-enactments of those in the past. One thinks immediately of the flights from responsibility in the novel—Ellis Burden walking out on Jack, Jack walking out on Lois, Hugh Miller deserting the Boss, Jack driving westward—and these withdrawals become symbolic repetitions of that larger, historical secession. Warren's novel implies that a division of time into past and present is no more valid than a separation between idea and fact, each of which should be either a source or extension of the other. Jack abandons his research on Cass Mastern when he begins to realize, as did Cass and as the modern South of both Stark and Stanton must also do, that the present is an extension of the past. Life or time, the novel seems to feel, is an unstoppable flood that acknowledges neither the pragmatist who feels the present is sufficient nor the escapist in his artifical womb.

II

Only when one is aware of the theme of division in the novel do Jack Burden's multitudinous theories yield to classification. Though Jack's philosophies are too numerous, and some of them too short-lived, to catalogue in full, his major theories fall into two categories: 1) those involving motion and hence, by implication, the flood; and 2) those that are basically escapist and that simulate the womb. As a philosopher, Jack is thus a schizoid: half of his theorizing is a sincere effort to explain what he feels he knows about life, but the other half is an attempt to rationalize his escapist tendencies. Jack's theories are thus a response to problems in the novel (to the theme of division, for example) as well as an extension of those problems. What one beholds in *All the King's Men*, then, is the struggle of a man seeking an explanatory framework for his experiences, a framework that he both needs and fears and that can resolve the novel if found.

As samples of Jack's womb or foetus theories one may point to the theory of brassbound Idealism and the concept of life as the Great Sleep. The first is a sort of perverted Platonism in which "if you are an Idealist it does not matter what you do or what goes on around you because it isn't real anyway" (p. 33). This is a very simple theory that allows Jack to pretend the real world and responsibility are illusory. In the Great Sleep, says Jack, one must regard sleep as a serious and complete thing, so that one gets up only in order to go back to bed. Jack retreats into the Great Sleep after leaving Lois and, earlier, after fleeing from the message that was starting to emerge from his doctoral dissertation. The Great Sleep is a response to life in which the death wish is implicit and the bed wherein Jack hides becomes a substitute womb.

Those of Jack's theories that involve motion—even if it is, at times, the motion of escapism and irresponsibility—still constitute a move towards the idea of the world as a flood or convulsion into which one must plunge responsibly. Two examples would be the idea of life as motion towards knowledge and the presentation of life as a process of heading West. To Ellis Burden Jack asserts that "Life is Motion toward Knowledge. God can't be Fullness of Being or Complete Knowledge or He'd be Non-Motion. Life is a fire burning along a piece of string (Ignorance, what we don't know) and the trail of ash is History, man's Knowledge." Insofar as it involves motion, the theory is positive, but knowledge functions here purely as a terminal point, never as a goal. The past becomes something that is used up. When the end of the string is reached, nothingness, or perhaps an explosion, results.

The idea of life as a process of heading West also amounts to an escapist theory. "For West," Jack writes, "is...where you go when you get the letter saying: *Flee, all is discovered*" (p. 286). Jack flees all the way to Long Beach after learning that Anne Stanton is Willie's mistress. This theory of life as movement westward is of interest because it prompts Jack to argue that "meaning is never in the event but in the motion through event." "Otherwise," Jack continues, "we could isolate an instant in the event and say that this is the event itself. The meaning. But we cannot do that. For it is the motion, which is important." There are positive implications here, such as the suggestion that the reality of an event may be a function of the relationship of that event to past and future events. Yet the main thrust of the theory seems designed to prevent anyone from pin-pointing the meaning of any particular event.

As a philosopher, then, Jack Burden is schizoid: one set of his theories deals with life as motion towards something, but another set seems concerned with an escape from life, with a recovery of the womb. The foetus or escape theories end in stasis, while the motion theories concede life is a process that one must be part of at the same time that they try to define the process in such a way that responsibility for one's actions is ruled out. If life is nothing but a Great Twitch, a meaningless, spasmodic phenomenon, as another Burden theory argues, then Jack need not wrestle with his burden, need not fuse past and present, idea and fact.

However, it is the theory of life as a Spider's Web, an idea formulated in Cass Mastern's journals and emphasizing responsibility, that demolishes most of Jack's other speculations and that gradually reveals itself as the structural principle underlying *All the King's Men.* Jack has been in search of a framework for experience and, as he finds it, the novel itself, as narrated by Jack, seems to share in the realization.

Cass Mastern's journals relate the story of his adulterous relationship with Annabelle Trice, the wife of his best friend. They also reveal the stages by which Cass learns the extent of individual responsibility. Cass concludes that Duncan Trice's suicide, the selling into prostitution of Annabelle's slave, Phoebe, and the loss by Annabelle of emotional and mental stability all come from the single sin of adultery "as the boughs from the bole and the leaves from the bough" (p. 189). To a Jack Burden who will later attempt to define life as goal-less motion, Cass' journals pose a serious threat and Jack must abandon the dissertation he is doing on them. It is only after he has resurrected Judge Irwin's past, indirectly forced the Judge to suicide, and learned from his mother that Irwin is his real father that the truth of Cass' Spider Web theory becomes irrefutable.

Cass learned, writes Jack towards the middle of the novel (p. 200), "that the world is *all of one piece.* [italics added] He learned that the world is like an enormous spider web and if you touch it, however lightly, at any point, the vibration ripples to the remotest perimeter." The idea of motion is present here ("the vibration ripples") but so too is the concept of responsibility and connection. It is not a starry-eyed, optimistic theory: the web can and, particularly in the cases of Cass and Irwin, does destroy. But in a novel full of characters each of whom seems to be two people and in which past and present, as well as idea and fact, seem irreparably separated, Mastern's theory re-asserts the awesome yet reassuring underlying unity of life. Motion in a straight line is not an adequate image for life; but motion along a series of interweaving lines is, Jack eventually feels, closer to the truth. The very fact that what was true for Mastern in the pre-Civil War period also holds true for Jack in the 1930's is a testimonial to that unity. Significantly, at the time Irwin shoots himself, Jack is asleep. At the sound of his mother's scream when she learns of Irwin's suicide, Jack recalls, "I came out of the sleep and popped straight up in bed. I was wide awake." It is clearly an awakening from a moral slumber. If "the world is all of one piece" as Mastern claims, then at least one, if not all, of the king's men, namely Jack, should be able to put it back together again, despite the terrible division of the age.

This is just what Jack, by chapter 9, claims to have done and what the structure or organization of the novel clearly reflects. Because he learned from Cass and from his own experience about the inter-relatedness of life and the prominence of responsibility, Jack is able to narrate the story of his years with Willie Stark. "I had been able," he writes, *"to gather the pieces of the puzzle up and put them to-gether to see the pattern"* [italics added] (p. 407).[10] He can formulate his theory about the split between men of idea and men of fact because he has attained a larger vision in which the unity behind the divisions and pieces is apparent. Now Jack can even explain his earlier misadventure with Anne and thereby, unlike the other in-habitants of Burden's Landing, accept the past and present as parts of a continuum. Anne trusted me, says Jack, as he re-examines his failure to make love to her, "but I did not trust myself, and looked back upon the past as something precious about to be snatched away from us and was afraid of the future. I had not understood then what I think I have now come to understand: that we can keep the past only by having the future, for they are forever tied together" (p. 329). The inhabitants of Burden's Landing who disassociate themselves from Willie Stark and, through him, from the modern world, are in need of this insight. If, argues Jack, you cannot "accept the past and its burden" (p. 461), there is no future. Once Jack has learned the truth about himself and his past and has concluded that life is a

[10]An extraordinary amount of modern fiction deals with the problem of putting past and present into meaningful relation. Proust, Joyce, and Faulkner are obvious examples, but, more particularly, Huxley's *Eyeless in Gaza* and Golding's *Free Fall* seem related to Warren's novel not only thematically but also in terms of structure. See John R. Strugnell, "Robert Penn Warren and the Uses of the Past," *Review of English Literature*, IV (October 1963), 93-102.

meaningful unity, he symbolically sheds his burden, since Burden is no longer his real surname (he should be Jack Irwin, Judge Irwin's son). He can even accept the burden of nursing the dying Ellis Burden, the man he had always considered his father and whose eccentric yet occasionally persuasive ideas he can now tolerate, perhaps even comprehend.

There is, of course, no guarantee that Jack and Anne will survive their contemplated plunge, at the end of chapter 10, into the flood of the world. The chances of reunifying fact and idea on the public level seem even slimmer. Admittedly, Hugh Miller, the scrupulously upright lawyer who served as attorney general in the Boss' earlier terms of office, will probably reenter politics and Jack will work as his aide, but it is far from certain that these two former king's men can put the Humpty Dumpty that is the modern age together again. Miller's election, even if he runs for governor in place of Tiny Duffy, is hardly assured. Yet Jack's conclusions concerning the Spider's Web do receive support from the structure of Warren's novel. Obviously, the story has not been told in a straightforward fashion. In fact, the story-line, at first examination, seems to be in itself a sort of Humpty Dumpty that has shattered into several pieces.

The novel opens (and ends) in 1939, but chapter 1 soon moves back to 1936, the year of Jack's last trip with the Boss to Mason City, and subsequently flashes back even further to the time Jack first met Willie fourteen years before in 1922. The structure of the novel thus seems to echo the split in Willie as the gap between Willie the country boy and Willie the Boss is reflected in the shift in time from 1936 to 1922. The first chapter ends with the Boss commissioning Jack to discover something incriminating about Judge Irwin, but Jack does not start to look until chapter 4 and Irwin is not confronted with the results of Jack's probing until chapter 8. The various plot elements or story-lines in the novel are thus taken up one at a time, dropped, then picked up again. The focus shifts from 1933 at the start of chapter 3 to 1896 for an account of Ellis Burden's marriage. The next chapter leaps all the way back to 1864 for the story of Cass Mastern. Chapter 6 is set mostly in 1937, but the following chapter recounts Jack's adolescence, his failure with Anne, and the start of his haphazardly escapist existence. In short, because its stories are seemingly told in fragments—the Irwin story, for example, weaves in and out of the foreground—the novel at first appears to reflect the terrible division of the age and to justify Jack's contention that life is a meaningless, directionless twitch.

Jack's initial reaction to Cass' Spider Web theory, one remembers, is to state his own conviction that the world "was simply an accumulation of items, odds and ends of things" (p. 201). Jack seems to be telling his story in accord with this view and thus there is, initially, a tacit alliance between the book's structure, its progress, and the hero's philosophy. However, by the time Jack comes to credit the Spider Web theory, the various stories or plot lines in the novel have coalesced, so that Jack's final theory about the world's structure is substantiated by the novel's structure: both present life as a web wherein separations between fact and idea or past and present are revealed as illusory.

What, finally, can be said about Burden's narrative style? Can one isolate its unusual aspects and see them as reflections of thematic conflicts already mentioned? If one passes by Warren's attempts to write like Faulkner[11] and admits that Jack's prose is often an exaggerated journalese (half Walter Winchell and half Mickey Spillane),[12] what remains? The answer is a schizoid style that uses motifs and clichés to reduce life to meaningless, or at least ignorable, stereotypes but that simultaneously employs an unprecedented quantity of metaphors and similes by which Burden proves, probably unconsciously, that connection is the cardinal rule in life and in the web that he eventually decides is the ultimate metaphor for life.

Burden habitually reduces to a cliché whatever—be it person or place—threatens his initial convictions about the irrelevance of most things in life. He follows this procedure with any person or place that he cannot come to terms with or cynically dismiss. Adam Stanton, whose idealism both irritates and compels Jack, is continually referred to as "the Friend of His Youth." Ellis Burden, Jack's supposed father who walked out on his family, is always "the Scholarly Attorney." The present husband of Jack's mother always appears as "the Young Executive" and Lois, Jack's former wife is either "Lois the machine" or Lois the "Georgia peach." All the people whose existence or philosophy is problematic for Jack find themselves capsulated in an epithet that permits Jack to avoid regarding them seriously. Jack's mother, the person with whom he

[11]See Warren's use of abnormally long sentences, particularly in the opening pages; his fondness for a series of adjectives where one would do; and his use of hyperbolic exaggeration (in describing, for example, Sugar-Boy's feats behind the wheel).

[12]Journalese: Mixture of big words with slang, the tendency to overwrite consistently; Winchell and Spillane: references to the "big boys" with diamond rings on their fingers or to Sugar-Boy's .38 "under his left armpit like a tumor."

seems most uneasy throughout the novel, is always talked of only in terms of her face, "a damned expensive present" both for each of her successive husbands and for Jack, who would prefer a permanent father figure. Jack admires Judge Irwin but is engaged in exposing him, so Irwin's plantation becomes a place where the "cotton grows white as whipped cream and the happy darkies sing all day, like Al Jolson" (p. 229).

The best example of reduction involves Lucy Stark. Willie's wife is a woman whose honesty and fidelity Jack is tempted to admire and whose delusion, at novel's end, that she is raising Tom's baby he is forced to tolerate. But throughout most of the novel Jack refuses to confront realistically any person whose ideas or virtues challenge his escapist outlook. He therefore describes Lucy as the kind of woman "that makes you think of telling secrets in the gloaming over a garden gate when the lilacs are in bloom along the picket fence of the old homestead" (p. 64). This collection of cliché phrases—like the epithet "Scholarly Attorney" when it is repeatedly used—contains nothing inherently opprobrious but rather exaggerates goodness and wholesomeness to the point where parody results. At this point, a superior contempt is permissible and Jack can indulge in cynicism.

But Jack's style indefatigably makes connections, sometimes between the most unlikely objects, at the same time that it tries to render certain people and their ideas contemptible. Quite possibly, Burden's style has a density per page of similes and metaphors unequaled elsewhere in modern prose fiction narrative. (This becomes even less debatable if one counts what might be called hidden or subdued similes—the use of such phrases as "the kind of," "the way that," and "as though.") Everything seems to flow together. The Boss' car becomes a cross between a hearse and an ocean liner and has springs "soft as mama's breast." Tiny Duffy's face is like a cowpatty in a spring pasture. The best example, one with connections within connections, occurs when Jack notes that Lucy's face:

> seemed to smooth itself out and relax...*the way the* face of the chief engineer does when he goes down to the engine room at night and the big wheel is blurred out with its speed and the pistons plunge and return and the big steel throws are leaping in their perfect orbits *like* a ballet, and the whole place, under the electric glare, hums and glitters and sings *like* the eternal insides of God's head...(p. 38). [italics added]

Within one sentence Burden combines Lucy's facial expression with that of a chief engineer, with the operations of an engine room, with the perfect harmony of a ballet, and, finally, with the mental processes of God. Working contrary to the theme of division, then, is a style that insists on unity through combination. The sentence quoted above is not unlike a spider's web. Any one fact or idea leads to an almost infinite series of related facts and ideas.

Jack's prose style is thus schizoid in that it insists on the interconnectedness of phenomena at the time that it talks about the division of an age or undermines the meaningfulness of life by its often cynical tone and its use of clichés. Furthermore, the split between Willie and Adam, a separation of idea and fact, also functions in Jack's prose as Jack is both romantic and crass, lyrical and colloquial. He can call his reclining body "the horizontal tenement of clay" and lament, when he learns Anne is Willie's mistress, that the last breath of spring has gone. But he can also report that the girl in the Mason City drugstore who first recognizes Willie "got a look on her face as though her garter had busted in church." The extent to which Burden is both Adam and Willie can be seen from the fact that he writes not only the way Adam the romanticist might write but also the way the Boss actually talks. Jack is in romantic territory when he describes Willie as "the margin of mystery where all our calculations collapse, where the stream of time dwindles into the sands of eternity...where chaos and old night hold sway and we hear the laughter in the ether dream" (p. 22). But he also notes, in language more suited to the Boss, that Willie "got his front feet in the trough" after his election and that spray comes from Sugar-Boy's mouth "like Flit from a Flit gun."

Throughout *All the King's Men*, the theme of "the terrible division of an age" influences characterization, structure, and style. The split between Willie and Adam finds its extension in many of the other characters who seem to be two people. It also finds its extension in the very structure of the novel, a structure that forsakes a straightforward story line for a fragmented approach. And, finally, it finds extention in the divergent moods and tendencies of Jack Burden's prose. Although the novel presents certain problems, particularly one of focus, its style and structure not only reflect its themes but assist in its resolution. What Jack learns about the nature of life is corroborated by the spider's-web structure the novel finally attains and by the strongest, most insistent aspect of Jack's style: its high content of metaphors and similes that link and unify.

Adam's Lobectomy Operation
and the Meaning of
All the King's Men

by James C. Simmons

> ...I have a story. It is the story of a man who lived in the
> world and to him the world looked one way for a long time
> and then it looked another and very different way. The
> change did not happen all at once. Many things happened,
> and that man did not know when he had any responsibility
> for them and when he did not. There was, in fact, a time
> when he came to believe that nobody had any responsibility
> for anything.... But later, much later, he woke up.[1]

Robert Penn Warren's *All the King's Men* is primarily a novel
of one man's search for self-realization, culminating in the development of his moral awareness and his acceptance of individual
responsibility. Jack Burden, the narrator, stumbles through his
life, searching for Truth, the discovery of which he hopes will explain why people are as they are and act as they do. He is a product
of the "terrible division of the age," torn by the conflict between
what the world appears to be and what he wants it to be, between
experience and innocence, between action and idea. He rejects the
doctrine of original sin embraced by his employer, Governor Willie
Stark, yet, finding himself thrust into the midst of political corruption and violence, he is too perceptive to deny the existence of

"Adam's Lobectomy Operation and the Meaning of *All the King's Men*"by James
C. Simmons. From *PMLA*, 86, (1971), pp. 84-89. Reprinted by permission of the
Modern Language Association of America and the author. Copyright © 1971 by
the Modern Language Association.

[1]Robert Penn Warren, *All the King's Men* (New York, 1953), p. 461. Subsequent
references from this, the Modern Library edition, are included in the text. I should
also like to acknowledge a debt to Diane Eisenberg, Roberta Fischkes, and Susan
Leeds, former students of mine at Boston Univ., whose insights into the novel have
found a place in this article.

evil altogether. Attempting to seek solace in such abstract theories
as idealism and mechanistic determination, he remains unsatisfied.
The novel is a search into the true nature of man and evil; and the
prefrontal lobectomy operation is strategically placed so as to provide specific insight into Jack's dilemma.

Adam's operation is significant for several reasons. On one level
Warren clearly intends an analogy between Jack Burden and the
anesthetized patient who in a very real sense is Jack's double, a
grotesque reflection of certain crucial aspects of his own character.
By forcing the confrontation, Warren in a brilliant stroke achieves a
parody of portions of the novel's larger action, recapturing in
symbolic form Jack's life and attitudes while simultaneously offering implicit criticism of that life and those attitudes. Jack's encounter with the catatonic schizophrenic is then an encounter with
himself, and his failure to see himself and his plight in the condition
of the patient becomes a measure of that same plight and his own
self-willed blindness. Warren further utilizes the scene to illuminate
the meaning of Jack's flight west and the subsequent adoption of
the mechanistic theory of the Great Twitch. And, finally, by its
very nature the operation stands as a symbolic representation of the
theme of division so pervasive throughout the book and, in retrospect, may be viewed as one step toward the resolution of this conflict. I shall now deal with each of these points individually.

I

Adam's patient is suffering from catatonic schizophrenia, the
symptoms of which are a typical pattern of gradual withdrawal from
reality, the sudden loss of animation, a tendency to remain motion-
less for long periods of time, some degree of emotional apathy, and
periods of stupor alternating with those of intense activity. As Adam
puts it to Jack: "The way he is now he simply sits on a chair or lies
on his back on a bed and stares into space. His brow is creased or
furrowed. Occasionally he utters a low moan or an exclamation.
In some cases we discover the presence of delusions of persecution.
But always the patient seems to experience a numbing, grinding
misery" (p. 336).

Jack displays these symptoms of catatonia throughout the novel.
The most pronounced is his persistent withdrawal, real or imagined,
from his immediate environment. Much earlier he had observed
that "The world was full of things I didn't want to know" (p. 151)

and imaged this condition in terms of a "clammy, sad little foetus you carry around inside yourself...its eyes are blind, and it shivers cold inside you for it...wants to lie in the dark and not know, and be warm in its not-knowing" (pp.11-12). Here Jack's comfort lies in his nonbeing, his impersonality, his complete disassociation from people. And later, shortly before he learns of Anne Stanton's affair with Willie Stark, Jack looks out from his office window and down into a nearby grove of trees and wishes himself "inside that hollow inner chamber, in the aqueous green light, inside the great globe of the tree, and not even a jay-bird in there with me now...and no chance of seeing anything beyond the green leaves" (p. 281).

The physical manifestations of these various impulses of retreat and withdrawal are Jack's four periods of the Great Sleep, a near-catatonic state in which lethargy dominates a large portion of his time:

> Lots of nights I would go to bed early, too. Sometimes sleep gets to be a serious and complete thing. You stop going to sleep in order that you may be able to get up, but get up in order that you may be able to go back to sleep...you are aware of it every minute you are asleep, as though you were having a long dream of sleep itself, and in that sleep you were dreaming of sleep, sleeping and dreaming of sleep infinitely inward into the center.   (p. 107)

The Great Sleep, an integrated part of Jack's personality, has over-taken him at four separate times in his life: upon the completion of his dissertation on Cass Mastern, the disintegration of his marriage with Lois, his resignation from his job as a newspaper reporter, and finally his realization of Anne Stanton's affair with the Governor. In each instance Jack makes a strategic retreat into the security of a dreamless sleep away from those periodic intervals of tremendous personal stress too painful for him to confront. And each time he lapses into this womb-like state of not-knowing, becoming com-pletely withdrawn and refusing to acknowledge both other people and himself, his condition is similar to catatonia.

Significantly, Adam performs his operation shortly after Jack's return from the West Coast and his most recent bout with the Great Sleep. Adam's explanation of the typical behavioral patterns of the catatonic schizophrenic stands as a remarkable summary of Jack's experience in California. There he had withdrawn into a Long Beach hotel room and slept for thirty-six hours. He also had his hallucinations: "as soon as I shut my eyes to go to sleep the whole hot and heaving continent would begin charging at me out of the dark" (p. 287). Adam's patient "lies on his back on a bed and stares into space" (p. 336); and Jack in his hotel room "lay on the bed, with my light off, watching the neon sign across the street flare on and off again to the time of my heartbeat" (p. 287). He, too, has his "delusions of persecution," seeing Anne's affair as a "betrayal" and deciding that she had never loved him in the first place, but only "had a mysterious itch in the blood and he was handy and the word *love* was a word for the mysterious itch" (pp. 327-28). Furthermore, like the catatonic schizophrenic, he experiences a "numbing, grinding misery." As Jack puts it: "Then I didn't feel anything. I didn't even feel sorry for myself. I felt as wooden as a wooden Indian" (p. 284). And finally those thirty-six hours of immobility and stasis are sandwiched in between the frenzied, excited drives to and from the West Coast, times of extreme motion; again this sudden fluctuation between extreme stasis and extreme activity is symptomatic of the catatonic schizophrenic.

II

The character of Jack Burden in the passage treating the lobectomy operation is consistent with the Jack Burden we have come to know from the beginning. He is the newspaper reporter: the detached, curious, distant, and accurate observer of events, the aloof commentator who falls back on his flippant and sarcastic wit to maintain the distance and keep himself uninvolved. His impulsive curiosity—"I felt all of a sudden that I had to see it. I had never seen an operation" (p. 336)—manifests itself throughout the novel. This "plain curiosity," reflected in his interest in Cass Mastern and all his various "digging" jobs for Willie Stark, is always exclusive of himself; he remains uninvolved, and his curiosity excludes any situation or person which obviously threatens introspection.

However, this is also the Jack who has just returned from his flight to the West with a new concept of the "Truth"—a theory of mechanistic determination that he calls "The Great Twitch," or the accident of circumstance. This is his "secret knowledge," his "mystic vision," that allows him to feel "clean and free" (p. 334). Jack's symbol of the Great Twitch, reducing, as it does, all actions to independent phenomena, unrelated in any way to any other phenomena in the world, is the extreme antithesis of Cass Mastern's image of the cobweb, denoting interdependence and interresponsibility, so that "if you touch it, however lightly at any point, the vibration ripples to the remotest perimeter" (p. 200).

Such a philosophy, of course, serves the immediate function of releasing Jack from the mixed emotions of guilt and love, his growing awareness of his own complicity in the affair of Anne Stanton and Willie Stark. It enables him to escape the confrontation with himself and the growing sense of guilt over Anne's seduction: "somehow by an obscure and necessary logic I had handed her over to him. That fact was too horrible to face, for it robbed me of something out of the past.... So I fled west from the fact, and in the West ...I had discovered the dream" (p. 329). Thus, Jack's trip to Long Beach and his subsequent theory of the Great Twitch are, in actual fact, merely other escape mechanisms and the new "vision" a more sophisticated form of the Great Sleep.

Jack's new interest in the lobectomy and his narration of the operation reflect his new vision. The lobectomy in one sense stands as the perfect demonstration of his theory of the Great Twitch, offering as it does the means of radically changing a man's personality by mechanical means; indeed, it is a test of that theory which holds man to be merely "a complicated piece of mechanism" and, by extension, conceives of the human personality as something existing in a dimension where it can be directly altered by "an electric curling iron." Thus, for Jack at this point every aspect of man, including his personality, exists on the same plane of being; that is, the "cutting" of the personality is not to be considered as anything really different from the removal of a gallstone (or a ball bearing). Furthermore, his description of the operation in terms of the disassembly and reassembly of a complicated machine reflects precisely the fundamental ramifications of the theory of the Great Twitch. Adam works with "a contraption like a brace and bit," and then a "Gigli saw" in order to get through the skull to "the real mechanism inside." It is all "high-grade carpenter work," Jack concludes from his vantage point in the pit, and he easily forgets that "the thing on the table was a man" (p. 337).

Various details of the operation suggest Jack's own conversion, which was also traumatic and sudden, and from which he emerged an advocate of the "secret knowledge" of the Great Twitch. The doctors work in "white nightshirts" over the anesthetized patient, recalling Jack on his West Coast hotel bed drowsy with sleep and Scotch. They drill a series of "burr holes" in the man's skull; and earlier Jack lay on his bed "with an electric fan burring and burrowing away into my brain" (p. 335). In effect, during his thirty-six hours in California and his espousal of the philosophy of the Great Twitch, Jack has experienced a symbolic lobectomy. And certainly Adam's diagnosis of the positive effects of the operation are an effective description of Jack after his trip: after a successful lobectomy the patient would be "relaxed and cheerful and friendly. He will smooth his brow. He will sleep well and eat well and will love to hang over the back fence and compliment the neighbors on their nasturtiums and cabbages. He will be perfectly happy" (p. 336). After Jack's "cure," he finds his depression eased and returns from Long Beach in "good spirits," coolly complacent in his new knowledge of the Great Twitch. He is more relaxed, cheerful, and friendly than on the trip out, picking up the hitchhiker in New Mexico on his way back, mixing sociably with the people in Stark's office (smiling "benignly like a priest"), and is, in short, "perfectly happy." But his contentment and his relationships with other people are, like those of the patient, unnatural and superficial. The patient's felicity and gregariousness are products of another man's skill, artificially induced, and empty of all emotional involvement. Similarly, Jack's "happiness" and socializing are based on a denial of empathy and a stiff suppression of all emotions. He has accepted the notion that relationships are dangerous when they become too emotionally involved. The pain he received from Anne resulted because he allowed her to get too close to him; he let her affect him as a person. To assure that no one will ever hurt him again, Jack disengages himself from all meaningful personal relationships, seeking a state of "invulnerability."

Jack's theory of mechanistic determination effectively increases his distance and remoteness from people through a process of dehumanization, that is, by seeing people and their actions in terms of random impulses of electricity throbbing through the muscle tissue, as sequences of mindless, meaningless, unrelated stimuli that provide an automatic response. This aspect is clearly reflected in the machine imagery used by Jack in his narration of the operation. The result of treating people as machines (precisely what the Great Twitch theory does) is identical to that of his symbolic catatonia. Both attitudes induce impersonality and noninvolvement and thus serve to negate Jack's chances for the realization of his total personality through a meaningful social relationship. His statement that "the man there on the table didn't seem real. I forgot that he was a man at all, and kept watching the high-grade carpenter work" (p. 337) suggests an attitude toward others little different from that displayed earlier in his account of his marriage to Lois, a relationship described, significantly, in similar terms. There, too, he tried to separate Lois the person from Lois the machine, and have a relationship only with the latter, assuring himself of an impersonal, dehumanized involvement and keeping himself aloof and invulnerable. "As long as I regarded Lois as a beautiful, juicy, soft, vibrant, sweet-smelling, sweet-breathed machine for provoking and satisfying the appetite (and that was the Lois I had married), all was well" (pp. 321-22). But when he began to think of her as a human being, conflict set in, and Jack found his comfortable seclusion compromised. His response was the catatonic Great Sleep and eventual flight, foreshadowing his later reaction to the discovery of Anne's affair with Stark:

> It was bracing because after the dream I felt that, in a way, Anne Stanton did not exist. The words *Anne Stanton* were simply a name for a peculiarly complicated piece of mechanism which should mean nothing whatsoever to Jack Burden, who himself was simply another rather complicated piece of mechanism. At that time, when I first discovered that view of things…I felt that I had discovered the secret source of all strength and all endurance. (p. 329)

However, Jack's encounter with Anne Stanton after the operation suggests the limitations to his theory and his own inability to make his private life match the principles of the Great Twitch. Clearly, Anne is not merely a "particularly complicated piece of mechanism which should mean nothing whatsoever to Jack Burden," when he murmurs to her, "'My dear, my dear,'…Then as I seized her hands pressed around the glass, the words wrenched out of me, 'Oh, Anne, why did you do it?'" (pp. 344-45). And with this initial admission that Anne is much more to him than a mere piece of machinery comes the first tentative and halting acceptance of his own guilt in the matter, something that moves him still farther away from his California vision that negated all sense of individual responsibility and thus abolished guilt. "I knew why she had done it. The answer was in all the years before, and the things in them. The answer was in me, for I had told her" (p. 345).

One salient idea here is that of self-definition in terms of others. Jack's major fear is that of self-knowledge: his disassociation from others is, in effect, an escape from himself.

> They say you are not you except in terms of relation to other people. If there weren't any other people there wouldn't be any you because what you do, which is what you are, only has meaning in relation to

other people. That is a very comforting thought when you are in a car in the rain at night alone, for then you aren't you, and not being you or anything, you can really lie back and get some rest. It is a vacation from being you.   (pp. 136-37)

Implicit in the above meditations is the idea of Jack as a product of "the terrible division of the age" (p. 462), reflecting that division constantly, not only in his "family reunions" with his other self (p. 137), but also in his pronounced tendency to view others as divided and disintegrated individuals.

Jack's continual flight from involvement is then, finally, a flight from himself and self-knowledge. From his fear of self-awareness he dehumanizes others, and thus, in effect, dehumanizes himself. Jack holds himself back from viewing the patient on the operating table as a human being because, should he do so, he would then be forced to view himself in the same light, and this would necessitate coming to terms with himself. In the opening pages of the novel Jack had voiced the fear that he enacts in the operating room: "The end of man is knowledge, but there is one thing he can't know. He can't know whether knowledge will save him or kill him" (p. 12). Throughout Jack lacks the courage to take that chance. Therefore, years before he had dropped his investigation into the history of Cass Mastern when he realized that implications could be drawn and applied to himself.

As long as Jack remains coldly detached, clinically analyzing the proceedings in the operating room, his mechanistic theory prevails. However, he finds himself unable to maintain the desired distance throughout the entire operation:

> I did fine until they started the burning...At first it wasn't so bad, but then I knew where I had smelled an odor like that before. It was the night, long back when I was a kid, when the old livery stable had burned down at the Landing, and they hadn't managed to get all the horses out.... As soon as I realized that the burning brain had a smell like the burning horses, I didn't feel good.   (pp. 337-38)

This reaction is significant for two reasons. It foreshadows Jack's eventual dissatisfaction with the mechanistic theory of the Great Twitch by demonstrating his response to the sudden realization that the brain and the man are alive. Significantly, the response is an emotional one, and, like that aroused by Anne a short time later, contradicts the code of the Great Twitch. Secondly, it is appropriate that it is a childhood memory that thwarts the theory, for Jack is a man haunted by the past to such an extent that he is incapable of acting in the present or planning for the future. At this point he is aware of the past but paralyzed by it, unable to understand or accept it. It is highly appropriate, then, that an event from out of the past should intrude upon and interfere with the present philosophy, which is in itself a negation of the past and its influence on the present.

For Jack, ultimate participation in the present and the opportunity for a full and rich life come only when he achieves a reconciliation with the past. His reaction to the childhood memory of the livery stable suggests what this acceptance of the past entails. At this point, he is unable to cope with the past, here the fire, for several reasons. There is a subconscious sense of guilt on his part over his inability to help the horses after he had sensed a feeling of responsibility toward them. He feels guilty as he recalls "the shrieks that horses had made" because he had failed to act independently and rescue them. In order for Jack to accept the past, he must recognize that he is a member of a large, unified family (the meaning of Cass Mastern's vision of the cobweb). As a child and during the operation, he is unable to identify his relationship and responsibility to the horses. As a man, Jack must confront the fact that he is a part of a family and must actively care for its members. Only through the rediscovery of the past is a reconstruction of the present possible, and with this a spiritual rebirth into life.

This theme of rebirth is, of course, basic to Warren's novel. Immediately after the lobectomy operation Jack baptizes the patient, "'for he is born again and not of woman'" (p. 338). In one sense there is a fundamental truth hiding behind his sarcasm; the man, in effect, has experienced a rebirth but, as Warren makes clear, this is an aborted rebirth, a death-in-life existence. But it does represent, in terms of the novel's symbolic analogy in this section, one possible alternative for Jack.

Jack is not, of course, the only individual in the novel to experience a rebirth. This is also true of Willie Stark, who during his first campaign for the governorship had been "blundering and groping his unwitting way toward the discovery of himself, of his great gift" (p. 388). His first speech, after learning from Sadie Burke that he had been a dupe of the Harrison machine, is a measure of his new knowledge—about himself and his world; and the result has been the birth of a new man, a new personality.

And once more we find ourselves returning to the lobectomy

scene. As Jack himself says much earlier in the novel, "the story of Willie Stark and the story of Jack Burden are, in one sense, the same story" (p. 168). And this idea is reiterated here in the narration of the operation. That the patient stands symbolically for both Jack Burden and Willie Stark is perhaps suggested by the initial description of the man on the table, who reminds Jack "vaguely of Andrew Jackson or a back-country evangelist" (p. 337), terms perfectly applicable to Willie Stark. This is not to suggest that Willie, like Jack, consistently displays the symptoms of the catatonic schizophrenic. Nevertheless, Willie's experiences in the twenty-four hours following his discovery of the true nature of things are, for all practical purposes, traumatic enough to produce a new personality and a new set of values. The talented "surgeon" in this case is Sadie Burke who works on Willie's "head" with the "tools" of sarcasm and blunt truth: "'Listen, if you can get this through your thick head. They wanted you to split the MacMurfee vote.... Can you get that straight, you wooden-head?'" (p. 87). Willie's immediate response to the news is severe shock followed by a withdrawal into the catatonic state of a drunken stupor. This action, of course, suggests the response typical of Jack's confrontations with the unpleasant moments in his life, but with this major difference—Willie's retreat from reality is only temporary, a matter of a few hours at most; Jack's is fundamental to his whole life.

Jack's narration of the operation includes details of "the little pieces of brain which had been cut out [and] put away to think their little thoughts quietly somewhere among the garbage, and what was left inside...was sealed back up and left to think up an entirely new personality" (p. 338). The "little pieces of brain" suggest the old personality that must be cast off in one way of another before rebirth is possible. The morning following his encounter with Sadie Burke, Willie is sick—"I puked'" (p. 93)—and in a sense this is analogous to the small bits of brain. This is what he leaves behind in the garbage of the hotel room, the old Willie, Cousin Willie from the country, as he sets out for the fair where he will assume his new personality.

Adam tells Jack that the operation would be a failure if the patient emerged from it cheerfully amoral. And this is what happens to Willie, who emerges from his "operation" at the hands of Sadie Burke as politically amoral, working with a philosophy of the ends justifying the means. His "operation," then, was a failure; he has metamorphosed into the antithesis of his former self.

III

In summation, we can say that the entire lobectomy scene poses the question of whether or not man is responsible for evil, whether, in fact, the philosophy of the Great Twitch is valid. In the closing line of the episode, Jack admits that "from the height of my Olympian wisdom, I seemed to find a great many things funny which now do not appear quite as funny" (p. 319). Thus, he informs us that the Great Twitch was merely a phase he passed through in his search for Truth. But, in retrospect, it is interesting that he employs the word "Olympian" to describe his acquired knowledge at that moment, for Olympus was the home of the Greek gods who had no moral responsibility and were, by the nature of their divinity, outside of Time and human affairs. Jack will be forced, by the sequence of events to follow, to recognize his human ties and, having done so, he will be able to "go into the convulsion of the world, out of history into history and the awful responsibility of Time" (p. 464). The image of the divided man, suggested by Adam's prefrontal lobectomy, will have been replaced by that of the connecting web of mutual guilt and responsibility.

Humpty Dumpty and *All the King's Men:* A Note on Robert Penn Warren's Teleology

by James Ruoff

Since the Pulitzer Prize novel *All the King's Men* (1946) is coming to be recognized as the most comprehensive statement of Robert Penn Warren's philosophy and art,[1] it might be worth while to remark upon a very general misconception regarding the title of the novel. Now, ordinarily, of course, a title is not a matter of any great significance, but in this case it is important because it constitutes a symbolic expression of some of the author's basic ideas. It is, in fact, a Pandora's box which opens up to reveal the profoundly spiritual nature of Warren's convictions about the broad themes of man and God; and once we have properly understood the title in its relation to the context of the novel, we shall be in a position to see exactly what the author intended when he remarked recently of *All the King's Men:* "The book...was never intended to be a book about politics. Politics merely provided the framework story in which the deeper concerns, whatever their final significance, might work themselves out."[2]

According to the generally accepted interpretation, "the King" in *All the King's Men* is the protagonist Willie Stark, an interpretation which derives from the fact Willie is governor of the state, a man the other characters in the novel refer to as "the Boss." "The King's

"Humpty Dumpty and *All the King's Men:* A Note on Robert Penn Warren's Teleology" by James Ruoff. From *Twentieth Century Literature* 3 (1957), 128-34. Reprinted by permission of the author and the publisher.

[1]See James Magmer, "Robert Penn Warren's Quest for an Angel," *Catholic World,* CLXXXII (1946), 178-83; Robert White, "Robert Penn Warren and the Myth of the Garden," *Faulkner Studies,* III (1954), 59-67; J. Letargeez, "Robert Penn Warren's Views of History," *Revue des Langues Vivantes,* XXII (1956), 533-43.

[2]Introduction, *All the King's Men* (Modern Library, 1953), vi. All quotations are from this edition.

Men," on the other hand, are assumed to be all the people who in one way or another serve the Boss—Jack Burden, Willie's research man; Tiny Duffy, the lieutenant governor; Sugar-Boy, Willie's bodyguard, etc. Then, too, there are "the King's women," the mistresses of the governor's palace—Sadie Burke, Anne Stanton, Willie's wife Lucy. As tidy as this interpretation undoubtedly is, something more than a casual reading of the story will show Willie Stark was never intended to be "the King" in *All the King's Men,* and that the title of the novel has a meaning more significant than critics have hitherto realized.

There are a number of reasons why Willie Stark cannot be "the King" in *All the King's Men.* There is, first, the nursery rhyme from which the title was derived: Willie is Humpty Dumpty, not "King." Like Humpty Dumpty, Willie "sat on a wall" when he rose to become governor and "had a great fall" when shot down by Adam Stanton. Willie is, like his legendary counterpart, a synthetic creation, a grotesque composite of the abstract needs of the people who have shaped him. As Warren has pointed out, Willie's "power was based on the fact that somehow he could vicariously fulfill the secret needs of the people about him."[3] Hence the principal characters in *All the King's Men,* like Mr. Munn in Warren's *Night Rider* (1939), attempt to find themselves by merging their identities with another person. In Willie Stark the people of the state satisfy their craving for justice—hence Willie's easy political slogan "Your need is my justice"— while to the narrator, Jack Burden, Willie fulfills Jack's need of a father, his need of the purpose and direction and decisive authority which have been lacking in his aimless life. To Adam Stanton, "the man of idea" who eventually destroys him, Willie represents the concrete power to accomplish the idealistic, humanitarian good which Adam has dedicated his whole life to achieve. In short, it is an obvious truism to say that to Sadie Burke, to Anne Stanton—to virtually every character in the novel—Willie Stark represents the fulfillment of some secret compulsion, some indigenous shortcoming or incompleteness, and in this sense, most of all, Willie is Humpty Dumpty—an artificial composite of the needs inherent in the society which has created him. After Willie's assassination Tiny Duffy performs the futile ritual of attempting to put Humpty Dumpty "back together again" when he seeks to employ Jack Burden, Sadie Burke, and Sugar-Boy, Willie Stark's political aides.

But if Willie Stark is Humpty Dumpty, who then is king? In view of the nursery rhyme it is difficult to see how Willie can be Humpty

[3]*Ibid.,* i.

Dumpty and king, too. Part of a solution to our problem is to be found in Warren's introduction to the Modern Library Edition, where he states that in *All the King's Men* he tried to "avoid writing a straight naturalistic novel, the kind of novel the material so readily invited." By the phrase "straight naturalistic novel" Warren apparently intended the bleakly deterministic and materialistic novel which portrays its characters as being merely biological organisms attracted and repelled by hereditary or environmental forces over which they have no control. As we shall see, the "material" of *All the King's Men* "readily invited" a novel of this description, for there is a temptation to think of Willie Stark as an ineluctible demi-urge riding the beast of the people to their moral collapse while the rider himself is pulled to destruction by a gloomy necessity. And yet one of Warren's main problems in writing *All the King's Men* was, I think, to avoid any implications of determinism, to establish a sure balance between the fact of Willie's diabolic attraction for others and the fact of their free wills; for it was essential to Warren's moral purpose, to his whole concept of man, that his characters exercise free will, that Willie Stark remain, after all, only Humpty Dumpty and not king—not Necessity, not God. In Warren's teleology only God is King, and we are all of us "all the King's men."

God is not only King but absolute monarch informing every moment of life with His purposive Will, and this predestination, which under Warren's hand becomes something quite different from determinism of a theological order, is "the material" that "readily invited" what Warren calls "the straight naturalistic novel," the novel which, in the tradition of Zola and Crane and Dreiser, is informed by biological necessitarianism and psychological behaviorism. This naturalistic tradition is emphatically repudiated in *All the King's Men* when determinism, a chief characteristic of "the straight naturalistic novel," is sardonically labeled "The Big [sic] Twitch" by Jack Burden, who abjures it as totally inadequate to explain the events that take place in the story. The philosophy Jack Burden does come to accept, however, is one which has to do with the enigmatic paradox of Christianity—the omnipotence of God and the moral responsibility of man. And if at the end of the novel Jack's acceptance of this view of life is not without some reservations, we must remember that the paradox is baffling, is one that derives not from a spontaneous rational acquiescence but from a hard discipline of faith.

If omnipotent God has power over everything, how can man be said to have responsibility for anything? *All the King's Men* confronts this question cautiously, with a full cognizance of the critical tensions created by Darwin, Marx, Freud, and the holocaust of two world wars. From these spirit-shattering, enervating experiences, we must preserve, Warren tells us, what is most distinctive, significant and compelling about man, his consciousness and spirituality. According to Warren, man has moral choice, lives in an "agony of will," but, paradoxically, he has no choice, no power whatever, in the consequences of his moral life. To put it another way, in Original Sin—which looms darkly in the background of all Warren's novels from *Night Rider* to *Band of Angels*—Adam and Eve devoured a fruit of agony when they ate of the Tree of the Knowledge of Good and Evil, for in that fatal act they took upon themselves the knowledge of what was right and wrong, and consequently the responsibility for their actions; but they were denied the divinity which Satan had promised them, the power to transcend time and perceive, as God perceives, the ultimate consequences of good and evil. (In Milton's *Paradise Lost,* for example, a travesty on those supernal powers promised to Adam and Eve by Satan is implicit when Michael comes to inform them of the Atonement, of the *real* consequences of the Fall which only God can know.)

Ironically, then, the Fall simultaneously gave man moral vision and struck him blind; it gave him an immediate, *a priori* knowledge of good and evil as it related to any moral decision, to any incoherent fact, but it left him blind to the ultimate purpose or direction or consequences of the fact. As an individual, he is the master of his soul in a moment of crucial moral decision; as a species, he is a pawn in a cosmic game the ultimate meaning or purpose of which he can never know. In *All the King's Men* Hugh Miller expresses the human viewpoint, indeed the only view man has capacity for, when he remarks at the end of the novel that "History is blind, but man is not."

This concept of history as a fleeting montage of seemingly purposeless causes and effects, of good and evil events so complex and confoundingly intermingled that man cannot perceive the *ultimate* good or evil of anything, is profoundly confirmed in *All the King's Men.* Several years before the story of Willie Stark unfolds, Judge Irwin accepted a bribe which Irwin's friend Jack Burden uncovers in one of his investigations as Willie Stark's research man. This bribe, a completely voluntary act, sets off a chain reaction of mediate causes and effects. First, her discovery that her father concealed Irwin's crime so disillusions Anne Stanton that she becomes Willie Stark's mistress, while her brother Adam so modifies his militant idealism that he agrees to accept Willie's offer of the directorship of the Willie Stark Memorial Hospital. When Adam learns of Anne's affair, he assassinates Willie. But Irwin's bribe has even more far-reaching consequences. Jack's discovery of the bribe leads to Irwin's suicide, to Jack's realization that Irwin is his real father, to a reconciliation of Jack and his estranged mother. Was Judge Irwin's crime an evil? Although Warren is neither a weak-headed immoralist nor a sentimental relativist, his answer remains ambiguous. For his crime Irwin suffers guilt, repentance, absolution by atonement, just as do the other characters, whose particular crimes have been the indirect result of Irwin's: Jack Burden for uncovering Irwin's bribe, Anne Stanton for her adulterous relationship with Willie, Sadie Burke for her malicious jealousy of Anne and betrayal of Willie, and Lucy Stark for her pride of virtue and weakness of mind. Irwin's crime is evil because it results in the destruction of Willie, of Adam, of Irwin himself, and yet it has the undeniably good effects of saving Mrs. Burden's soul, of uniting her with her son, of bringing together Anne and Jack, and finally — if the reader chooses to remain skeptical of Willie's death-bed assurance that "things might have been different" — of freeing the people of the state from the grip of an unscrupulous demogogue. Hence Judge Irwin's crime and its results confirm what Jack Burden describes as the "moral neutrality of history." As an isolated, incoherent fact it is evil, but as a part of history, as one stitch in a complex, variegated tapestry, it has shades of both good and evil.

Willie Stark expresses a profound truth when he insists throughout the novel that good must come from evil because "evil is all you have to work with," while Adam Stanton, the more conventionally "noble" of the two, lives a dangerous error when he arbitrarily separates people and events into moral categories. The point is made by Jack Burden at the conclusion of the story: "As a student of history, Jack Burden could see that Adam Stanton, whom he came to call the man of idea, and Willie Stark, whom he came to call the man of fact, were doomed to destroy each other, just as each was doomed to try to use the other and to yearn toward and try to become the other, because each was incomplete with the terrible division of their age."[4] Willie

---

[4]Page 462. In a recent article ("The Failure of Robert Penn Warren," *College English*, XXVIII [April, 1957], 359), Norman Kelvin argues that there is no basis for Warren's distinction between Willie as "the man of fact" and Adam Stanton as "the man of idea": "The Willy [sic] Stark we met in the novel was as much a man of ideas as was the puritanical, compulsive Dr. Stanton. They merely held to *different* ideas, and while some of Willie's were outrageous, so were some of Adam's." But this appears to be a very literal reading of what, after all, is only a pair of arbitrary metaphors. It matters not, really, what phrases Warren employs to describe Willie and Adam so long as we recognize his meaning.

brings about his own destruction when he tries to be like Adam, when, like "the man of idea" that he is not, he sets out to create something which is completely devoid of evil. Inconsistent with his own philosophy that any good there is must come from evil, Willie dreams of building a magnificent hospital that will stand as the purely good achievement of his political administration, and yet, unknown to Willie, the hospital is tainted by evil in the moment of its conception, for the idea of the hospital is really the result of Willie's unconscious effort to compensate for the guilt he feels in protecting from prosecution his corrupt state auditor, Bryam B. White. The hospital becomes an instrument of Willie's downfall when he refuses to permit the venal Gummy Larson from having the contract to construct it, when he refuses, in other words, to allow the good he dreams of achieving to be contaminated by evil, and this refusal prompts Tiny Duffy to inform Adam of Willie's affair with Anne. In shooting Willie Stark, Adam becomes himself "the man of fact," acknowledging Willie's dictum that the end justifies the means, but more than that, he proclaims by his act that he has God's knowledge, a final knowledge of good and evil. In his arrogant effort to usurp divinity, Adam repeats the folly of the Fall.

The fact that Willie's hospital is never built underscores man's tragic limitations. Confined to a tenuous reality of isolated facts, hemmed in by illusory absolutes of good and evil, man cannot perceive the transcendent reality, the ultimate moral purpose and direction of life. Willie, "the man of fact," thinks he knows how things really are, and Adam Stanton, "the man of idea," thinks he knows how things ought to be, but both are incomplete, both presumptuous. So man lives on one moral level of reality, where he suffers an "agony of will," of personal responsibility, and God exists on another, the level of "history" or "direction," a level unknown to man, who yearns toward the fulfillment of some ideal good which in the "moral neutrality of history" has no objective existence.[5] On God's level, good and evil are not as inseparable as man persists in making them. What man conceives as a completed moral action is, in God's omniscient comprehension, merely another phase in man's continuous struggle to create some good in a fallen world he

[5]In a very interesting article ("The Meaning of Robert Penn Warren's Novels," *Kenyon Review,* X [Summer, 1948], 417), Eric Bentley describes Warren as "utterly empirical." This is of course true; nevertheless, Professor Bentley does not appear to be sufficiently aware of how in Warren's novels the facts of experience and Christian orthodoxy coalesce. Of how, in other words, empiricism confirms Warren's essentially Christian philosophy of life.

only faintly understands. Warren's concept of man as a fallen, debased, limited, and therefore heroic, creature working out moral decisions in an "agony of will" yet oblivious to the eventual good or evil of those decisions is one which recalls St. Augustine and medieval nominalists like Duns Scotus (the analogues of Warren's Puritanism), who stressed God's awful power and mystery, and man's irrationality and impotence. Like these medieval nominalists who reacted against the liberal rationalism of the Scholastics, Warren has repudiated the optimistic rationalism of the liberal reformers, just as he has repudiated their scientism and materialism—what Jack Burden refers to as "the dream of our age."

In *All the King's Men* man finds solace not in the liberal experience, not in the nineteenth-century dream of power through reason, but in the more ancient Christian experience of humility, repentance and hope; for Warren sees this world as a Dantesque purgatory where man works out his salvation by a process of transgression, acknowledgement of guilt, and contrition. Every character in *All the King's Men* who is worth saving eventually submits to this tortuous ritual of life: Cass Mastern, Judge Irwin, Willie Stark, Jack Burden, Mrs. Burden, Sadie Burke, and Anne Stanton. Tiny Duffy, like his friend Gummy Larson, is a mere shade, an abstraction, while Adam Stanton, paradoxically the "noblest" character in the novel, is, by the fact of his fierce and intransigent pride in virtue, quite beyond all hope of redemption. For the remainder of the characters in *All the King's Men,* however, the epigraph to the novel applies. Appropriately, the epigraph to *All the King's Men* is Manfred's tortured cry of hope in Canto III of Dante's *Purgatorio:* "Mentre che la speranza ha fior del verde."

As if to turn back at the end of the novel to interpret his story, Warren spells out these ideas about God and man in a religious tract dictated to Jack by Ellis Burden:[6]

> The creation of man whom God in his foreknowledge knew doomed to sin was an awful index of God's omnipotence. For it would have been a thing of trifling and contemptible ease for Perfection to create mere perfection. To do so would, to speak truth, be not creation but

[6]Page 462. I am not suggesting that Ellis Burden is a mouthpiece through which Warren expresses his views, nor that this religious tract is a violation of the novel's dramatic integrity. Ellis Burden is a fully developed, integrated character, and his tract does have a certain dramatic inevitability. Nevertheless, Ellis Burden, and to a less extent perhaps, Hugh Miller, function in a way reminiscent of a Sophoclean chorus: they may have their etiology in Warren's pseudo-Greek drama *Proud Flesh,* which, written in 1938, was the germinal beginning of *All the King's Men.*

extension. Separateness is identity and the only way for God to create, truly create, man was to make him separate from God Himself, and to be separate from God is to be sinful. The creation of evil is therefore the index of God's glory and His power. But by His help. By His help and in His wisdom.

Jack Burden tentatively concurs in Ellis Burden's credo. "I did so to keep his mind untroubled," he says, "but later I was not certain that in my own way I did not believe what he had said." Jack's statement, although not an unqualified affirmation, is nevertheless a long step away from his earlier cynicism and philosophical determinism. It signifies a gradual awakening of Jack's spirituality, the beginning of an unconscious application of Cass Mastern's story to his own tragic experience in life. In his diary, which Jack had studied but could not understand until his own experiences confirmed its views, Cass Mastern had written: "I do not question the Justice of God, that others have suffered for my sin, for it may be that only by the suffering of the innocent does God affirm that men are brothers in His Holy Name" (p. 199). Cass Mastern sees the world as a vast spider web of intersecting lives:

> Your happy foot or your gay wing may have brushed it ever so lightly, but what happens always happens and there is the spider, bearded black and with his great faceted eyes glittering like mirrors in the sun, *or like God's eye*, and the fangs dripping. (Italics mine, p. 200.)

Because the Cass Mastern episode was printed as an independent story before the publication of *All the King's Men*, some critics have been quick to regard it as an extraneous feature, as a brilliant but irrelevant *tour de force*, and yet, as Eric Bentley has pointed out, it is really Warren's effort to "put the whole theme of a work into one short and strongly symbolic interlude."[7] It supplies not only an inverted contrast to Jack's own story, a contrast between a crime of commission and one of omission, but plainly underlines the dominant themes of the omnipotence of God, and the utter helplessness and brotherhood of men. Cass Mastern tripped the gossamer threads of the spider web when he seduced his best friend's wife; Judge

---

[7]"The Meaning of Robert Penn Warren's Novels," 415-16. It ought to be mentioned, however, that the Cass Mastern episode is not completely successful. For one thing, it invites comparison with the adulterous relationship between Irwin and Mrs. Burden rather than with the Platonic romance of Jack and Anne. Hence at the end of the novel Warren felt it necessary to have Jack Burden point out that Judge Irwin bears no resemblances to Cass Mastern: "For Judge Irwin and Cass Mastern do not resemble each other very closely. If Judge Irwin resembles any Mastern it is Gilbert, the granite-headed brother of Cass." (p. 464)

Irwin when he accepted the bribe; Willie Stark when he refrained from prosecuting Bryam B. White; and Jack Burden when he revealed the truth about Irwin. That Jack comes to accept Cass Mastern's view of the world is suggested when he observes toward the end of the story that "each of us is the son of a million fathers" (p. 462), but more pointedly, when Jack, who has always been lashed by a compulsion to seek and reveal the truth, tells his mother an outright lie rather than impart to her the cause of Irwin's suicide, and when he lies to Sugar-Boy rather than name the man who was indirectly responsible for Willie Stark's death. On both occasions Jack's prevarication, like Marlow's lie to Kurtz's Intended in Conrad's *Heart of Darkness,* is an honest man's acknowledgement and atonement. Now sharing Cass Mastern's vision of the world as a web of humanity, Jack dares not assume responsibility for awakening the drowsy spider. He has come to see the brotherhood of men and the universality of guilt.

To assume, then, that Willie Stark is "the King" in *All the King's Men* is to ignore the meaningful symbolism of the title, to lose sight of Warren's basic idea. As I have attempted to show, *All the King's Men* portrays a world which Willie could not have ruled; for in that world of Warren's thoughtful creation there is but one King and we are all of us "all the King's men." From first to last, Willie Stark is but Humpty Dumpty, whose fall is a form of triumph for those who survive him. As Ellis Burden states in another context, "Separateness is identity," and with the death of Willie those who involved their identities in him must find completion within themselves or not at all. As in any great tragedy, there is loss, there is gain: they have lost Willie but have gained the power to find themselves. It may not be a coincidence, therefore, that the conclusion to *All the King's Men* is reminiscent of the ending to another great tragedy as Jack Burden and Anne Stanton, like Adam and Eve departing from the Garden after the Fall, prepare to leave Burden's Landing forever to "go into the convulsion of the world, out of history into history and the awful responsibility of Time."

Introduction to the Modern Library Edition
of *All the King's Men*

by Robert Penn Warren

Some time in the winter of 1937-38, when I was teaching at the
Louisiana State University, in Baton Rouge, I got the notion of
doing a verse play about a Southern politician who achieved the
power of a dictator, at least in his home state, and who was assassinated in the Capitol which had been the scene of his triumphs. As
well as I can recall, the notion began to take on some shape when,
sitting one afternoon on the porch of a friend's cottage, I began to
describe my intentions.

Very often it is in conversation during the germinal stage of a
project that I stumble on my meanings, or they stumble on me, and
I recall this particular conversation rather vividly because it was
then that I hit on the idea that the politician—then unnamed—would
not simply be a man who by force or fraud rises to absolute power,
offends the principles of decency and democracy, and then is struck
down by a self-appointed Brutus. There would be no drama to such
a story—no "insides," no inner tensions, no involvement of the
spectator's own deep divisions. My politician would be—or at least
I was groping toward some such formulation—a man who in many
ways was to serve the cause of social betterment, but who was corrupted by power, even by power exercised against corruption. That
is, his means defile his ends. But more than that, he was to be a man
whose power was based on the fact that somehow he could vicariously fulfill some secret needs of the people about him. The choruses—
and it was in talking about the place of the choruses in the proposed
verse play that the notion came—were to develop this in a subsid-
iary way—a chorus of builders, a chorus of highway patrolmen, a
chorus of surgeons, etc. And, naturally, each of the main characters
should bear such a relation to the politician, even the Brutus assas-

sin. But over against his power to fulfill, in some degree, a secret need of those about him, the politician was to discover, more and more, his own emptiness and his own alienation. So much for that conversation in the unseasonable sunshine of a Louisiana winter day.

The play did get written. I wrote a couple of choruses in the next few months. In Italy, the next summer, the summer of 1938, I got a little more done, beginning the process, I recall, in the late afternoon, in a wheat field outside of Perugia. The thing dragged on all the next winter and spring, in Louisiana, with a bit done after classes and on week-ends, but the bulk of the play was written in Rome, in the fall and winter of 1939, with the news of the war filling the papers and the boot heels of Mussolini's legionaries clanging on the stones. During that time I was deep in Machiavelli and Dante. Later, in the novel *All the King's Men,* Machiavelli found a place in the musings of Jack Burden, and Dante provided the epigraph.

When the play was finished, it was somewhat different from the thing dreamed up in the conversation with my friend. For instance, another theme had crept in — the theme of the relation of science (or pseudo-science) and political power, the theme of the relation of the science-society and the power-state, the problem of naturalistic determinism and responsibility, etc. At least, if such grand topics did not find explicit place in the play, and if I did not pretend to wisdom about them, they were casting a shade over the meditations of composition. The play, by the way, had the title *Proud Flesh.* I was rather pleased with the double significance of the phrase.

I mailed off the play to some friends back home. I knew that it was not finished, but I would postpone the rewriting for the benefit of the judgment of my first readers and my own more detached contemplation. Back in America, in the summer of 1940, I did do some rewriting, with the subtle criticism and inspiring instruction of Francis Fergusson. But still the play was not, to my mind or taste, finished. And besides, I had already begun a novel, to appear as *At Heaven's Gate,* which was drawing on some of the feelings and ideas involved in the play.

It was not until the spring of 1943 that I began again on the play. I had taken the manuscript out of its cupboard with the intention of revising it, but immediately I found myself thinking of the thing as a novel. That idea wasn't entirely new. Now and then I had entertained the possibility of making a novel of the story. But now, all at once, a novel seemed the natural and demanding form for it, and for me.

This new impulse was, 1 suppose, a continuation of the experience of writing *At Heaven's Gate*, just as that novel had been, in a way, a continuation of *Proud Flesh*. Despite important contrasts, there were some points of essential similarity between my businessman hero, Bogan Murdock, in *At Heaven's Gate*, and the politician hero of the play. And even some of the contrasts between them were contrasts in terms of the same thematic considerations. For example, if Bogan Murdock was supposed to embody, in one of his dimensions, the desiccating abstraction of power, to be a violator of nature, a usurer of Dante's Seventh Circle,* and to try to fulfill vicariously his natural emptiness by exercising power over those around him, so the politician rises to power because of the faculty of fulfilling vicariously the secret needs of others, and in the process, as I have already said, discovers his own emptiness. But beyond such considerations, the effort of *At Heaven's Gate* had whetted my desire to compose a highly documented picture of the modern world — at least, as the modern world manifested itself in the only region I knew well enough to write about.

There was, however, another consideration, if one can use such a term of scruple and calculation to describe the coiling, interfused forces that go into such a "literary" decision. This consideration was a technical one — the necessity for a character of a higher degree of self-consciousness than my politician, a character to serve as a kind of commentator and *raisonneur* and chorus. But since in fiction one should never do a thing for merely a single reason (not if he hopes to achieve that feeling of a mysterious depth which is one of the chief beauties of the art), I wanted to give that character a dynamic relation to the general business, to make him the chief character among those who were to find their vicarious fulfillment in the dynamic and brutal, yet paradoxically idealistic, drive of the politician. There was, too, my desire to avoid writing a straight naturalistic novel, the kind of novel that the material so readily invited. The impingement of that material, I thought, upon a special temperament would allow another perspective than the reportorial one, and would give a basis for some range of style. So Jack Burden entered the scene.

But that is not quite a complete account of his origin. In *Proud Flesh*, at the time when Dr. Adam Stanton is waiting in the lobby of

---

*It was this Circle that provided, with some liberties of interpretation and extension, the basic scheme and metaphor for the whole novel. All of the main characters are violators of nature.

the Capitol to kill the Governor, and is meditating his act to come, an old friend, now a newspaperman, approaches him, and for one instant the assassin turns to him with a sense of elegiac nostalgia for the innocence and simplicity of the shared experiences of boyhood. This character, who appears so fleetingly in the last act of the play to evoke the last backward look of the dedicated assassin, gave me Jack Burden. And the story, in a sense, became the story of Jack Burden, the teller of the tale.

The composition of the novel moved slowly, in Minneapolis, in 1943 and through the spring of 1944, in Washington through the rest of the year and up till June of 1945, in Connecticut in the summer of 1945. The work was constantly interrupted, by teaching, by some traveling, by the duties of my post in Washington, by the study for and writing of a long essay on Coleridge. The interruptions were, in some way, welcome, for they meant that the pot had to be pushed to the back of the stove to simmer away at its own pace. The book was finished in the fall of 1945, back in Minneapolis, the last few paragraphs being written in a little room in the upper reaches of the Library of the University of Minnesota. The book, after a good deal of revision along the way, with the perceptive criticism of Lambert Davis of Harcourt, Brace and Company, was published in August, 1946.

One of the unfortunate characteristics of our time is that the reception of a novel may depend on its journalistic relevance. It is a little graceless of me to call this characteristic unfortunate, and to quarrel with it, for certainly the journalistic relevance of *All the King's Men* had a good deal to do with what interest it evoked. My politician hero, whose name, in the end, was Willie Stark, was quickly equated with the late Senator Huey P. Long, whose fame, even outside of Louisiana, was yet green in pious tears, anathema, and speculation.

This equation led, in different quarters, to quite contradictory interpretations of the novel. On one hand, there were those who took the thing to be a not-so-covert biography of, and apologia for, Senator Long, and the author to be not less than a base minion of the great man. There is really nothing to reply to this kind of innocent boneheadedness or gospel-bit hysteria. As Louis Armstrong is reported to have said, there's some folks that if they don't know, you can't tell 'em.

But on the other hand, there were those who took the thing to be a rousing declaration of democratic principles and a tract for the assassination of dictators. This view, though somewhat more congenial to my personal political views, was almost as wide of the mark. For better or for worse, Willie Stark was not Huey Long. Willie was only himself, whatever that self turned out to be, a shadowy wraith or a blundering human being.

This disclaimer, whenever I was callow enough to make it, was almost invariably greeted by something like a sardonic smile or a conspiratorial wink, according to what the inimical smiler or the friendly winker took my motives to be—either I wanted to avoid being called a fascist or I wanted to avoid a lawsuit. Now in making the disclaimer again, I do not mean to imply that there was no connection between Governor Stark and Senator Long. Certainly, it was the career of Long and the atmosphere of Louisiana that suggested the play that was to become the novel. But suggestion does not mean identity, and even if I had wanted to make Stark a projection of Long, I should not have known how to go about it. For one reason, simply because I did not, and do not, know what Long was like, and what were the secret forces that drove him along his violent path to meet the bullet in the Capitol. And in any case, Long was but one of the figures that stood in the shadows of imagination behind Willie Stark. Another one of that company was the scholarly and benign figure of William James.

Though I did not profess to be privy to the secret of Long's soul, I did have some notions about the phenomenon of which Long was but one example, and I tried to put some of those notions into my book. Something about those notions, and something of what I felt to be the difference between the person Huey P. Long and the fiction Willie Stark, may be indicated by the fact that in the verse play the name of the politician was Talos—the name of the brutal, blank-eyed "iron groom" of Spenser's *Faerie Queene,* the pitiless servant of the knight of justice. My conception grew wider, but that element always remained, and Willie Stark remained, in one way, Willie Talos. In other words, Talos is the kind of doom that democracy may invite upon itself. The book, however, was never intended to be a book about politics. Politics merely provided the framework story in which the deeper concerns, whatever their final significance, might work themselves out.

Willie Stark and Huey Long:
Atmosphere, Myth, or Suggestion?

by Ladell Payne

And truth was what I sought, without fear or favor, and let
the chips fly.   JACK BURDEN

In the twenty years since *All the King's Men* was published,
Robert Penn Warren has repeatedly denied that Willie Stark is a
fictional portrait of Huey Long. And by his own account, his denials
have been "almost invariably greeted by something like a sardonic
smile or a conspiratorial wink."[1] His two essays on the subject—an
"Introduction" to *All the King's Men* (1953) and *"All the King's
Men:* The Matrix of Experience" (1963)[2]—have certainly met with
the written equivalents of a smile, a wink and a nod. The most
notable early disbeliever was Hamilton Basso, whose "The Huey
Long Legend" seems to have prompted the 1953 disclaimer. After
describing the protagonists of Warren's *All the King's Men,* Dos
Passos' *Number One,* Langley's *A Lion Is in the Streets* and his own
Sun in Capricorn, Basso says: "He [Willie and the others collec-
tively] may not be intended to represent Huey Long, but it is hard
to see how he could represent anybody else," for "once a writer
begins to write about these Huey's-who-aren't-Hueys, the real Huey
jumps up and clings to his back like the old man of the sea."[3] Sub-

[1]"Introduction," *All the King's Men* (New York, 1953), pp. v-vi. All future references to *AKM* will be cited parenthetically in the text from this Modern Library
edition.

[2]*"All the King's Men:* The Matrix of Experience," *Yale Review,* LIII (1963),
161-67.

[3]"The Huey Long Legend," *Life,* XXI (Dec. 9, 1946), 108-10, 116.

sequently, Orville Prescott, in the course of attacking Warren's failure to see Stark as a step toward fascism, remarked that Willie is "obviously and closely modeled on Huey Long";[4] and such diverse writers as Louis D. Rubin Jr., David H. Zinman and William H. McDonald have echoed Basso and Prescott.[5]

Where, then, does the truth lie? In Mr. Warren's continued denials or in everyone else's continued suspicions? Of course, even Warren has readily admitted some relationship between Willie and Huey, acknowledging in 1953 that "it was the career of Long and the atmosphere of Louisiana that suggested the play that was to become the novel" and in 1963 that if he "had never gone to Louisiana and if Huey Long had not existed, the novel would never have been written." Even so, Warren has stood by his earlier position that "suggestion does not mean identity," and that because he did not know "what Long was like, and what were the secret forces that drove him,...Long was but one of the figures that stood in the shadows of imagination behind Willie Stark." And, in 1963, he reinforced this emphasis on the generally suggested at the expense of the specifically copied by differentiating the "world of 'Huey'—that world of myth, folklore, poetry, deprivation, rancor, and dimly envisaged hopes" from a "factual world—made possible by the factual Long." Warren's point is that Long became a legend in his own lifetime, and that by the time the novel was started in 1943, the "factual world was only a memory, and therefore was ready to be absorbed freely into the act of imagination."

[4]"The Political Novel: Warren, Orwell, Koestler," *In My Opinion: An Inquiry Into the Contemporary Novel* (Indianapolis, 1952), p. 25. One of the ironies of *AKM's* reception is that, while some thought the novel too flattering to Huey Long, members of the Long family seem to have resented the portrayal. Responding to Basso's "Legend," Mr. (now Senator) Russell B. Long said:

> I venture the assertion that no man of our time has been more abused, vilified, and misrepresented by the American press to its reading public than my father, Huey P. Long. Most commonly he has been accused of being a ruthless dictator who would have destroyed our system of democratic government as well with the charge as a noisy low-grade rabble-rouser [sic]. A mass of fictional novels pictures him as possessed of an obsessive lust for sexual indecencies. All glory in the fact that at law there is no right of suit by the decendants [sic] or relatives of a deceased man who has been libeled. ...As the son of the man, I must protest against such enormous misrepresentation (U.S. Congressional Record-Senate, 80th Cong., 1st Sess. 1947, XCIII, Pt. I, 438).

[5]Louis D. Rubin Jr., "All the King's Meanings," *Georgia Review*, VIII (1954), 422-23; David H. Zinman, *The Day Huey Long Was Shot: September 8, 1935* (New York,

There seems to be a significant difference between Warren's 1953 and 1963 statements: the early statement implies that Long's career and Louisiana's atmosphere suggested the novel's general plot and perhaps some of Stark's characteristics; the later statement says that Long and Louisiana simply inspired Warren with a "line of thinking and feeling," implying that Warren was concerned less with Long than with questions of public and private morality prompted by a mythical "Huey" and a metaphysical Louisiana that were recollected in the tranquillity of Mussolini's Italy and written about in Minneapolis, Washington and Connecticut.

While it is undoubtedly true that *All the King's Men* is not a literal biography of Huey Long, and equally true that much of the novel's literary value comes from the philosophical cogency of its subject matter—free will, determinism, human responsibility, the relationship between past and present—*All the King's Men* is much more directly based on the historical Huey Long than the words "suggested," "atmosphere," "line of thinking and feeling" and "world of myth" can possibly imply. Whether or not Warren tried "to transpose into fiction Huey P. Long and the tone of that world," the fact remains that he succeeded in doing so. For in the novel's sequence of events, in the subordinate characters and in the characterization of Willie himself, so much is drawn directly from the publicly-known career, cohorts and character of Huey Pierce Long that Warren's statements, while not false, nonetheless have been misleading. Moreover, while Warren's claim not to know Long's secret motives is of course literally correct, many of those who wrote about the historical Kingfish attributed motives to him very much like those of Warren's fictional Boss.

The story of Huey P. Long, an obscure southern farm boy who became governor of his state, went on to the United States Senate after acquiring dictatorial powers, and was assassinated at the height of his political career for reasons never fully known, is also the story of Willie Stark.[6] Like Long, Willie is a "red-faced and red-necked

---

1963), pp. 257-58; William H. McDonald, "A Summer Rerun on Warren's Powerful Novel," Montgomery (Ala.) *Advertiser-Journal*, July 24, 1966, p. 5A.

[6]General information about Long's career comes from the major studies published before Warren began his novel in 1943: Carleton Beals, *The Story of Huey P. Long* (Philadelphia, 1935); Forrest Davis, *Huey Long: A Candid Biography* (New York, 1935); Thomas O. Harris, *The Kingfish: Huey P. Long, Dictator* (New York, 1938); Harnett T. Kane, *Louisiana Hayride: The American Rehearsal for*

farm boy" (*AKM,* p. 7) from what had been the timber-producing part of a state that is obviously Louisiana. Taken together, the description of the sharp break between the flat rich country of the lower cotton delta and the low red hills of the poor upper-state region; the use of names such as Okaloosa for Opelousas, Marston for Ruston, Harmonville for Hammond, and Mason City for Morgan City; and the importance of oil in the state are things that can only refer to Louisiana.

In Winn Parish (county) of this state, young Huey Long supported himself by peddling shortening; young Willie peddles his Fix-It Household Kit by day while studying at night. Long's Baptist background and five months at the University of Oklahoma parallel Stark's year at a nearby Baptist college and his army time in Oklahoma. Long's fantastic achievement of learning enough law in eight months at Tulane to pass the bar examination becomes Willie's three-year period of rigorous night study. (This capacity for intensive work over extended periods later stands both Huey and Willie in good stead; both governors were able to go without sleep indefinitely when the occasion demanded.)

Willie Stark's early legal and political career also closely parallels Long's. Huey began with small-claims and workmen's compensation cases and became a well-to-do attacker of corporations; Willie begins with small claims, wins his first battle in a workmen's compensation case, and becomes financially independent attacking an oil company for some independent leaseholders. Long was elected to the railroad commission as the little man's champion and lost his power after he attacked Standard Oil for some independent oil companies. When we first see young Stark, he is a county treasurer fighting a corrupt admin-

Dictatorship (New York, 1941); Webster Smith, *The Kingfish: A Biography of Huey P. Long* (New York, 1933); Huey P. Long, *Every Man a King* (Chicago, 1964). Many specific details come from the first-hand studies of Hermann B. Deutsch: "Hattie and Huey," *Saturday Evening Post,* CCV (Oct. 15, 1932), 6-7. 88-92; "Huey Long of Louisiana," *New Republic,* LXVIII (Nov. 11, 1931), 349-51; *The Huey Long Murder Case* (New York, 1963); "Huey Long—The Last Phase," *Saturday Evening Post,* CCVIII (Oct. 12, 1935), 27, 82-91; "Paradox in Pajamas," *Saturday Evening Post,* CCVIII (Oct. 5, 1935), 14-15, 34-40; "Prelude to A Heterocrat," *Saturday Evening Post,* CCVIII (Sept. 7, 1935), 5-7, 84-88. I owe personal debts of thanks to Mr. Deutsch, who generously gave me a morning from a busy day; to Mr. Robert H. Fossum, who painstakingly criticized my manuscript; and to the librarians who staff the Department of Archives and Manuscripts and the Louisiana Room at Louisiana State University, the William B. Wisdom Collection at Tulane University, and the Louisiana Department at the Louisiana State Library.

istration and failing to win re-election because he opposes those in power. In describing the campaign for county treasurer, Warren gives Stark one of Long's political trademarks. As Huey did throughout his career, Willie distributes handbills from house to house because the local newspaper refuses to print his side of the story.

Huey used the notice he attracted on the railroad commission to run for governor; Willie runs for governor because of the attention he attracts as county treasurer. While Huey, unlike Willie, was certainly not tricked into entering the race, it remains true that each man failed in his first attempt at the governorship. Moreover, there is considerable evidence that Warren's picture of the young, idealistic Stark is drawn directly from some of young Long's characteristics. When Jack Burden first sees the Boss, he is country Cousin Willie, who refuses to drink beer, speaks politely, uses no profanity and wears a "stiff high collar like a Sunday-school superintendent" (*AKM,* pp. 16-21). According to Hermann Deutsch, until Long left Winnfield at sixteen, he was a devout churchgoer who used no profanity. Warren's description of Cousin Willie's "seven-fifty seersucker suit which is too long in the pants so the cuffs crumple down over the high black shoes, which could do with a polishing, and a stiff high collar...and a blue-striped tie" (*AKM,* p. 16) reproduces almost exactly a widely-published picture of Long as a traveling salesman in a rumpled suit, baggy pants and high collar, holding a sample case in one hand and an umbrella in the other. In 1963, Deutsch confirmed that young Long did indeed dress "like a misprint in a tailored-by-mail catalogue."

Nor is the older Willie Stark at all unlike the mature Huey Long. Willie is "five feet eleven inches tall and heavyish in the chest and shortish in the leg" (*AKM,* p. 16). His eyes are "big and brown, and he'd look right at you"; he has an "almost pudgy face," with "dark brown, thick hair...tousled and crinkled down over his forehead, which wasn't very high in the first place" (*AKM,* p. 21), and with jowls which are "beginning to sag off" (*AKM,* p. 8). According to Deutsch, Huey was also five foot eleven with a "tendency toward incipient paunchiness," with "reddish-brown eyes" and a habit of "staring at the person addressed as though seeking to hypnotize a subject." Basso notes Long's "fleshy face" and his "tousled reddish curls tumbled upon his forehead," and Hodding Carter remarks that he was "heavy-jowled."[7] Even Stark's informality in the governor's

---

[7]"Paradox," *Saturday Evening Post,* CCVIII, 14; Hamilton Basso, "Huey Long and His Background," *Harper's,* CLXX (May 1935), 664; Hodding Carter, "Louisiana Limelighter," *Review of Reviews,* XCI (Mar. 1935), 23.

office—conducting official business in his shirt sleeves and sock feet and settling "affairs of state through a bathroom door" (*AKM*, p. 32) —recalls Huey's habits of receiving dignitaries in shirt sleeves (at best) or green pajamas (at worst) and of occasionally standing stark naked while laying down the law to lesser politicians.

Cousin Willie's dull, platitudinous speeches, made up of "argument and language that was grand and bright" (*AKM*, p. 74), seem based on Long's early prose, that "florid and polysyllabic style he evidently admired most at that stage of his career."[8] From polysyllabic grandiosity, both Huey and Willie moved to the folksy, colorfully metaphorical language of their days in power—language filled with invective, invocative effects, and Biblical allusions and rhythms.[9] That Warren has drawn on Long's speeches is evident from only a few examples:

> *Huey.* We got the roads in Louisiana haven't we? In some states they only have the graft.[10]
>
> *Willie.* Sure, there's some graft, but there's just enough to make the wheels turn without squeaking. (*AKM*, p. 417)
>
> *Huey.* They want these pie-eaters and trough-feeders put out of control of the Democratic Party in Louisiana.[11]
>
> *Willie.* It is just a question of who has got his front feet in the trough when slopping time comes. (*AKM*, p. 417)
>
> *Huey.* Those low-down, lascivious, lying, murderous, bunch of skunks. Dog-faced sons of wolves.[12]
>
> *Willie.* Folks, there's going to be a leetle mite of trouble back in town. Between me and that Legislature-ful of hyena-headed, feist-faced, belly-dragging sons of slack-gutted she-wolves. (*AKM*, p. 155)
>
> *Huey.* Ladies and gentlemen, at birth the 'sugar-tit' of the state of Louisiana landed in L. E. Thomas's mouth.[13]
>
> *Willie.* Oh, I took the sugar tit and hushed my crying. (*AKM*, p. 101)
>
> *Huey.* The people...and not Huey Long, rule the State. Where are the schools that you have waited for your children to have, that have

[8] New Orleans *Item*, "The Kingdom of the Kingfish," Aug. 2, 1939, p. 1; "Speech and Platform of Huey P. Long," Long Scrapbook I, Z-5 # 1666 (Dec. 1923-Sept. 1925), p. 12, Department of Archives and Manuscripts, Louisiana State University.

[9] Expressing the opinion of many observers, Carleton Beals in "Sharing Vice and Votes," *Nation*, CXLI (Oct. 2, 1935), 377, called Long the "greatest 'Cain killed Abel ...go thou and do likewise' Bible quoter in America."

[10] George Sokolsky, "Huey Long," *Atlantic Monthly*, CLVI (Nov. 1935), 526.

[11] Harris, p. 36.

[12] John K. Fineran, *Career of a Tinpot Napoleon* (New Orleans, 1932), p. 170; Kane, p. 73.

[13] Beals, *Story*, p. 67.

never come? Where are the roads and the highways that you send your
money to build, that are no nearer now than ever before? Where are
the institutions to care for the sick and disabled?[14]

Willie. You are the state. You know what you need. Look at your pants.
Have they got holes in the knee? Listen to your belly. Did it ever
rumble for emptiness? Look at your crop. Did it ever rot in the field
because the road was so bad you couldn't get it to market? Look at
your kids. Are they growing up ignorant as you and dirt because there
isn't any school for them? (*AKM*, p. 97)

Huey. I know the hearts of the people, because I have not colored my
own.[15]

Willie. My study is the heart of the people. (*AKM*, p. 8)

The image of Willie making a speech—eyes bulging, face flushing,
sweat sluicing, arms flailing—has its source in Huey's platform
appearances, which consistently prompted the crowd, like Warren's
"rednecks," to respond as to a gospel preacher.

The patronizing contempt Tiny Duffy feels toward Cousin Willie
also is based on fact. The professional politicians clearly considered
Long something of a buffoon until it was too late to stop him. And if
Huey Long, unlike Willie Stark, underwent no great moral or spiritual change during or after his first campaign for governor, in their
second campaigns both Long and Stark relied much more on demagogic tactics and folksy language to win the necessary rural votes.

Long's later political career falls into five phases: his program of
public works and social reforms, his fight against impeachment, his
attainment of absolute power, his rise to national prominence as a
Senator and Share-Our-Wealth advocate, and his assassination. With
the exception of the Share-Our-Wealth program, Willie Stark goes
through all these phases. Moreover, he goes through all of them in
almost exactly the same way as did Long.

In *Every Man A King,* Long said that the most important parts of
his first legislative program were highway construction; free school
books; aid to the blind, deaf and dumb; and aid for the insane and
charity hospitals. To finance these reforms, he proposed to increase
the severance taxes on oil, gas, timber and other natural resources.
Stark, too, speaks proudly of his highway program, his public

[14]Louis Cochran, "The Louisiana Kingfish," *American Mercury,* XXVI (July
1932), 283; Long, p. 99.

[15]U.S. *Congressional Record—Senate,* 74th Cong., 1st Sess., 1935, LXXIX, Pt. III,
2953. This sentence and its context were widely quoted in Louisiana after the
assassination.

health bill, his extraction tax and his increased royalties on state land. Observers at the time recognized that the attempt to impeach Long was not to prevent wrongdoing, but to eliminate a political enemy. Warren makes it clear that the attempt to impeach Stark is for the same purpose. The Articles of Impeachment charged Long with, among other things, having "bribed and attempted to bribe legislators," having used "coercive measures," and with "high crimes and misdemeanors in office, incompetence, corruption, favoritism or oppression in office and gross misconduct."[16] Stark is charged with "attempting to corrupt, coerce, and blackmail the Legislature, in addition to the other little charges of malfeasance and nonfeasance" (*AKM*, pp. 154-55). Huey Long sped up and down Louisiana, making as many as seven speeches a day to gain support and calling for his followers to fill Baton Rouge on April 3. They crowded in for a massive night rally. Willie Stark roars "across the state at eighty miles an hour," attends "five, or six, or seven, or eight speakings in a day," and holds his mass rally "the night of the fourth of April" (*AKM*, pp. 155-59). Opponents accused Long of trying to bribe and coerce members of the Legislature to vote against impeachment; he is known to have driven as far as two hundred and fifty miles in the middle of the night to secure the support of a wavering senator; and by his own account, he simultaneously sent cars around to fifteen senators to get their votes. Willie Stark does all these things. And just as Governor Long escaped impeachment when his fifteen Round Robiners (one more than the number needed to block impeachment) anounced "that by reason of the unconstitutionality and invalidity of all impeachment charges remaining against Huey P. Long, Governor, they [would] not vote to convict thereon,"[17] so Governor Stark produces a list of signatures stating that "the impeachment proceedings are unjustified" and that the signers "will vote against them despite all pressure" (*AKM*, p. 159).

Evidently Long never experienced any transformation comparable to that effected in Willie by Duffy and Sadie. Nevertheless, the impeachment attempt profoundly disturbed him—even to the extent of weeping when the proceedings began. Afterward, his attitude toward his political opponents was noticeably harsher, his methods noticeably more cynical. In 1930, Long suggested this change: "I was governor one year before I learned that I had to be governor or

---

[16]Louisiana, "Calendar of the Senate Sitting as a Court of Impeachment," *Official Journal of the Proceedings of the Senate*, 5th Extra Sess., 1929, pp. 54-83.

[17]Long, pp. 169-70.

get out."[18] In August 1934, *Newsweek* quoted him as saying, "I was soft then...but not now, Brother." And in an interview reported by Forrest Davis, Long said: "When I got into politics I was just an ignorant boy from the country. All the political tricks I learned, I learned from them when they were trying to keep Huey P. Long out."

Stark and Long acquired and used their power in almost identical ways. Willie boasts of putting men on the Supreme Court to rule as he wants. The Articles of Impeachment charged Huey with using his appointive power to influence the state judiciary and with boasting of controlling the courts. Just as Willie announces to his followers that "there'll be a little something coming to you now and then in the way of sweetening" (*AKM,* p. 140), so Huey's supporters became judges and high-paid attorneys, and built homes with gold toilet fixtures. Willie forces his retainers to sign undated letters of resignation; the Articles of Impeachment charged Long with the same conduct. Jack Burden tells us that after Stark's election "there wasn't any Democratic Party. There was just Willie" (*AKM,* p. 103). Huey Long announced to the 1932 Democratic National Convention, "I am the Democratic Party in Louisiana."[19] And, just as Willie confidently imposes his will upon the state constitution to get the laws he wants, so Long announced once to a critic, "I'm the Constitution around here now."[20] Indeed, when Willie says, "The law is always too short and too tight for growing humankind. The best you can do is do something and then make up some law to fit" (*AKM,* p. 145), he is directly paraphrasing Long's "Unconstitutional? Hell, when I want something done I do it and tell my attorney general to dig up a law to cover it."[21] Surely Willie's explanation that the only way he can get things done is by using corrupt methods, however distasteful to him, sounds like Long's typical self-defense: "They say they don't like my methods. Well, I don't like them either. I'll be frank with you. I really don't like to have to do things the way I do. I'd much rather get up before the Legislature and say, 'Now this is a good law; it's for the benefit of the people and I'd like for you to vote for it in the interest of the public welfare.' Only I know that

[18]Clipping identified as being from the Shreveport *Journal*, Sept. 18, 1930, "Administration of Honorable Huey P. Long." Scrapbook in 7 volumes prepared by the office of Eugene A. Conway, Supervisor of Public Accounts, III, 37, Louisiana Department, Louisiana State Library; also see Davis, p. 119.

[19]*Review of Reviews,* XCI, 26.

[20]Kane, p. 64.

[21]U. P. Dispatch, Washington, Sept. 11, 1935, clipping identified as being from Scranton (Pa.) *Times,* Louisiana State University, Louisiana Room, Vertical Files.

laws ain't made that way. You've got to fight fire with fire."[22] True, Willie Stark does not become a national political figure. Yet toward the end of the novel, the Boss is planning to run for the Senate, and some of Willie's early, apparently facetious remarks at least suggest presidential ambitions (*AKM*, p. 43).

Stark's assassination, however, is obviously based upon Long's. Dr. Carl Austin Weiss shot Long in the Capitol building as he was leaving a night Senate session. Dr. Adam Stanton shoots Stark in the Capitol after the "solons had broken up shop for the evening and were milling about in the corridors" (*AKM*, p. 418). Long was walking between the Governor's office and private elevator in the east corridor leading from the Senate chamber; Stark is walking "along the east wall, toward the inset where the elevators were" (*AKM*, p. 420). According to Joe Bates, one of Long's bodyguards who testified at the inquest, "a man in white walked up to Senator Long. I thought he was going to shake hands. He shot him."[23] Other eyewitness testimony had Weiss stepping from behind a pillar. Jack Burden sees Stanton "leaning against the pedestal" of a statue. As Stanton approaches Willie, Jack thinks: *"He's shaking hands with him, he's all right now, he's all right."* Then Stanton fires. Weiss was killed at once by a hail of bullets—sixty-one wounds were counted in his head and body; Stanton was gunned down by a "positive staccato series of reports…. He was stitched across the chest" *(AKM*, pp. 420-21). Public Service Commissioner O'Connor (who commandeered a car and took Long to the hospital) said that "On his way to the hospital, Senator Long sat silently, pressing his hand to the bullet wound in his right side. Only once did he say anything, and that was to ask: 'I wonder why he shot me?'"[24] He had been shot once in the stomach by a small caliber pistol. Although an emergency operation was performed, Long died some thirty hours after the assassination. Governor Stark sits, "both hands pressed to his body, low on the chest and toward the center" with "two little .25-caliber slugs in his body." Willie also is taken to the hospital for an operation; a few days later, shortly before he dies, he turns to Jack and asks, "Why did he do it to me?" (*AKM*, pp. 421-24).

Even Willie's return to virtue shortly before his assassination seems directly based on Long's conduct. Just as Governor Stark

[22]F. Raymond Daniell, "The Gentleman from Louisiana," *Current History*, XLI (Nov. 1934), 172.

[23]Quoted by Zinman, p. 216.

[24]New Orleans *Times-Picayune*, Sept. 9, 1935.

drank heavily and chased "Nordic Nymphs," Governor Long "divided his time between government and dissipation," prompting Theodore Bilbo to speak of "Louisiana's pot likker governor's 'fondness for' liquor, women and green pajamas."[25] As he gained national prominence, Senator Long apparently tried to build a more favorable image of himself. George Sokolsky wrote that Huey gave up "a life-long habit of drinking heavily" a few months before his death. Hodding Carter observed the same change and noted that Long had toned down his rowdy conduct of the sort that Willie renounces when he returns to Lucy and tells Jack Burden "it might have been all different" (*AKM,* p. 425).

Fact and fiction also reflect each other in the figures who surround the Boss and his historical counterpart. As his Tiny Duffy, Huey had O. K. Allen, an incompetent, notable only for invariably supporting Long. Allen, according to one, "would have made a good hay, grain, and feed merchant in Halitosis, Louisiana." When Long was first elected to the Railroad Commission in 1918, O. K. Allen was Tax Assessor of Winn Parish. When Cousin Willie is serving his first term as County Treasurer in 1922, Tiny Duffy is Tax Assessor of Mason County. During his term as governor (1928-32), Long made Allen chairman of the Highway Commission; Stark gives Duffy the same job. Allen succeeded Long as governor of Louisiana in 1932 and served as the Kingfish's puppet; Duffy is the/Lieutenant Governor during Willie's last term and succeeds to the governorship after the assassination. As the man in Stark's organization most interested in graft, Duffy all too clearly resembles the Allen whose Highway Commission Long's enemies pointed to as the source of bribes and payoffs.[26] And though there is little physical similarity between the portly Allen and the obese Duffy, and no evidence to suggest that Allen had a hand in Long's assassination, Huey treated O. K. much as Willie Stark treats his principal sycophant. That is, Long apparently bullied and despised Allen. The October 13, 1932, issue of *Time* reported that "One day during the last legislative session, Senator Long called out roughly: 'Oscar, go get me those goddam bills we was talking about.' Governor Allen, embarrassed by the presence of others, pretended not to hear. Huey Long howled: 'Goddam you, Oscar, don't you stall around with me! I can break

[25]Harris, pp. 92-93; New Orleans *Morning-Tribune,* Mar. 17, 1931.

[26]Fineran, p. 3; Harris, p. 124; Sam Irby, *Kidnapped by the Kingfish* (New Orleans, 1932), p. 38; Shirley G. Wimberly, "Unmasking (Crawfish) Huey P. Long" (New Orleans: 21-page pamphlet, 1932), p. 6.

you as easy as I made you. Get those goddam bills and get them on the jump.' Governor Allen got them on the jump." At the 1932 Overton election-fraud hearings, Huey's brother, Julius, testified: "He makes all candidates sign undated resignations. I remember when he made Governor O. K. Allen sign one. The Governor broke down and cried." Julius added: "No man with the resentment of a bird dog would take what Oscar took from Huey Long." And Earl Long is the source of the story that when a leaf once blew in Allen's office window and fell on his desk, O. K. signed it.

If Tiny Duffy is a reasonably accurate portrait of O. K. Allen, then Sadie Burke, Willie's secretary, campaign assistant, and confidante, is clearly a modified picture of Alice Lee Grosjean, Huey's twenty-five-year-old secretary, campaign assistant, confidante, and eventually Secretary of State. While Sadie is not blessed with Alice Lee's beauty, their careers are remarkably parallel. Jack Burden's description of Sadie as "a very smart cooky" (*AKM*, p. 79) echoes Forrest Davis' characterization of Alice Lee as "the shrewdest 'man' of them all"; and Beals' comment that Alice Lee is "a girl who talks freely but reveals nothing, has been loyal to Huey, but stuck out for her own rights," fits Sadie equally well.[27] Moreover, the triangular relationship among Willie, Sadie and Lucy Stark seems noticeably similar to what was rumored to have existed among Huey, Alice Lee and Rose Long. When Governor Long appointed Miss Grosjean Secretary of State in 1930, *Time's* report (entitled "Long's Latest") was accompanied by a picture of Alice Lee captioned "Her Governor was good to her." During this year's campaign Terrell [Miss Grosjean's divorced husband] threatened to sue Governor Long for alienating his wife's affections. Mrs. Rose McConnel Long...does not regularly reside with her husband in the executive mansion at Baton Rouge or in his elaborate hotel suite in New Orleans. She remains at Shreveport where she says she prefers the schools for the three Long youngsters."[28] Sam Irby, Alice Lee's disreputable uncle by marriage, wrote that she "told me that she had quarrelled with her mother, who had accused her of impropriety in her relation with her employer, and had demanded that she and her husband leave her home." Irby adds: "The next I heard of them was when I learned that a divorce had been agreed upon and arranged by Huey Long who first asked Mr. Terrell to sign a statement to the effect that Long was not responsible for the separation." Irby also says pointedly

[27] Davis, second page of an unnumbered "Postscript"; Beals, pp. 192-93.
[28] *Time*, XVI (Oct. 20, 1930), 19.

that Huey's and Alice Lee's "living quarters were on the same floor of the Heidelberg Hotel."[29]

There is, of course, no indication that Alice Lee colluded in the assassination. But Sadie's withdrawal to a sanatorium at the novel's end and her confession—"Oh God...Oh, God...I killed Willie. I killed him." (*AKM,* p. 435)—may have been suggested by a widely believed false rumor. In 1936 Cleveland Deer, the anti-Long candidate for governor, asserted that one of Long's bodyguards, then in a mental institution, kept muttering to himself: "I've killed my best friend! I've killed my best friend!"[30]

While Mrs. Rose Long was perhaps not as saintly as Lucy Stark, the two are similar in many ways. Lucy's retreat to a poultry farm parallels Mrs. Long's separate residence in Shreveport. Lucy's willingness, for appearance's sake, to pose for photographs is analogous to Mrs. Long's brief stints as hostess at the governor's mansion. And Mrs. Stark's qualities are the same as those one writer recognized in Mrs. Long: "courteous and thoughtful, gentle in speech, and kind to all associates."[31] Rose Long's Leibnitzean belief that "everything works out for the best" and that the "justification of a life is in good works"[32] could well be attributed to Lucy Stark. Even the close relationship between young Willie and Lucy seems to reflect that between young Huey and Rose during their Tulane days when, "for the first, last, and only time in his life, Huey P. Long...lived withdrawn from the world. Absorbed in each other, he and his young wife embarked upon the project of seeing how quickly a three-year law course could be mastered."[33] Finally, Lucy's repeated affirmation that Willie "was a great man" is remarkably like Mrs. Long's statement that her husband "was the greatest man who ever lived."[34]

Sugar-Boy, Willie's stuttering, fast-driving, sharpshooting, dim-witted, absolutely devoted bodyguard appears to be a composite of two of Long's protectors, Joe Messina and Murphy Roden. Most of Sugar-Boy's personal traits come from Messina, Long's chief body-guard. While Messina did not drive for Long, he had been a truck

[29]Irby, pp. 22-23.

[30]Quoted by Deutsch, *Murder Case,* p. 139.

[31]H. O. Thompson, U. P. Correspondent, syndicated series of six articles published shortly after Long's death, Louisiana State University, Louisiana Room, Vertical Files.

[32]F. Raymond Daniell, "Mrs. Huey Long Emerges, Modestly," *New York Times Magazine,* Feb. 9, 1936, p. 11.

[33]"Heterocrat," *Saturday Evening Post,* CCVIII, 84.
[34]*New York Times Magazine,* Feb. 9, 1936, p. 11.

driver at one time, and as Long once put it, could "shoot out a bird's eye at a hundred yards." Messina's stupidity was common knowledge. One person told me of seeing him spend a day clutching campaign money in a paper bag as a child would clutch a bag of candy. Davis reports meeting him in an outer room spelling out the "balloons" in the comics, much as Jack Burden meets Sugar-Boy looking at a picture magazine. Although Messina did not stutter, his simpleminded attempt at the impeachment trial to explain why he was on the state payroll without admitting he was a bodyguard seems a kind of mental if not physiological stutter. Furthermore, Sugar-Boy behaves very much like Messina during and after Long's assassination. At the inquest, Messina was at first incoherent, then wept, and finally testified: "I ran up, pulled my gun and emptied it at the man who shot Senator Long.... I killed him because he had killed Senator Long."[35] At the assassination, Sugar-Boy fires repeatedly at Dr. Stanton and then leans over the fallen Willie "weeping and sputtering" (*AKM*, p. 421).

Murphy Roden, a crack shot who also fired at Weiss, was Long's regular driver. While there is no evidence that Long's car ever wiped "the snot off a mule's nose" (*AKM*, p. 5), it did come "down Canal Street like a gulf squall...its rear end slewing to the gutters."[36] Even Sugar-Boy's hostility toward the "B-b-b-b-as-tuds" who fail to get out of the way as fast as he wants, while perhaps not based specifically on either Messina or Roden, reflects the general hostility of Long's bodyguard corps toward those who did not make way for their charge.

Of all the characters who surround the Boss, Jack Burden is by all accounts not only the most important to the novel but the hardest to pin down to any prototype. Hamilton Basso says that "Long did have a sort of research man, a former journalist who printed his findings in Huey's personal newspaper, *Louisiana Progress*. It does not appear, though, that Mr. Warren, in creating the character of Jack Burden, had him in mind." Basso is presumably referring to John D. Klorer, who edited the *Progress* from its founding in 1930 until about nine months after Long's assassination; but if research is the characteristic that identifies Burden with Klorer, a much stronger case can be made for Warren's drawing this quality from Long himself. Certainly Jack Burden's habit of keeping "a little

[35]New Orleans *Times-Picayune,* Sept. 16, 1935.

[36]Walter Davenport, "How Huey Gets Away With It," *Collier's,* June 17, 1933, p. 10.

black book" full of essential information was suggested by "a little black book that all Louisiana knew and feared—Huey's 'sonofabitch book.' Anybody who had ever done him a wrong…was there."[37] It is conceivable that Basso himself was the model for Burden, since in 1935 Basso wrote of his experience on a New Orleans opposition newspaper, of his pleasure in seeing Long win the governorship, of his belief in the sincerity of the early Long, of the value of Long's many social reforms and of his conviction that "Huey is a possible good against a positive evil. It is a choice between Huey and the New Orleans' gang, and Huey is simply the better choice to make."[38] Then, too, Earle J. Christenberry, Senator Long's private secretary (described by Deutsch in 1963 as one of Long's "two closest friends") might have suggested Burden. But there is little substantial evidence for the contention that Warren had Christenberry or Klorer or Basso or even Long specifically in mind when he created Burden. Instead, Burden seems the one of Stark's close associates who was "suggested by" a knowledge of Long and his cohorts rather than closely modeled on any one of them. And rightly so. For by creating a wholly fictional narrator who not only chronicles and comments on the factually-based Willie Stark story, but who himself has a past, present and future that constitutes a major portion of the novel, Warren has legitimately and successfully accommodated the world of fact within the world of fiction. For within the context of Jack Burden's experience, historical matter takes on the form of fiction.

Carl Weiss, while not one of Long's associates, is forever linked to him as his assassin. And Warren's Dr. Adam Stanton is recognizably like Dr. Carl Austin Weiss. Miss Louise Garig, Weiss' former English teacher at Louisiana State University, wrote and sent a moving eulogy to several newspapers after the assassination.[39] She pictured the doctor as a thoughtful, good, kind, cheerful, almost saintly man. Harris, too, described Weiss as "gentle, peaceloving, pious and filled with hope and ambition for the future.··.a cultured and greatly beloved young doctor." Stanton has all these attributes. The New Orleans *Item* reported on September 10, 1935, that "music was [Dr. Weiss'] relaxation and he took it seriously, studying in his spare time." Adam Stanton plays the piano both for relaxation and

[37]Kane, p. 62.

[38]*Harper's,* CLXX, 671.

[39]A typescript of this statement, along with correspondence between Miss Garig and Mrs. Carl Austin Weiss, is in the New Orleans Public Library, Louisiana Room, Vertical Files.

as a symbol of his frustrated desire for harmony in a chaotic world. As the idealistic man who wants only "to do good" (*AKM*, p. 252), Stanton might well be the man described by Weiss' mother in a widely published statement about her son: "All we know is that he took living seriously. Right with him was right. Right above everything." Indeed, even the deliberate contrast Warren draws between Stanton, the man of idea, and Stark, the man of fact, may have been prompted by comments at the time. One southern editorialist wrote: "Huey Long is dead. He died by the hand of a man who was his direct opposite in every human trait."[40] Finally, while Stanton's motives are clearly stated in the novel (as, of course, they must be) and while we can only speculate about Dr. Weiss' (as we have to in real life), both assassins seem to have been impelled by an insult to family or honor rather than by strong political feelings.

If Weiss' motives remain conjectural, so too do Long's. A number of people, however, believe that the forces which produced and motivated Willie Stark were also those which gave rise to and moved Huey Long. Warren indicates that Willie is the product of what happened in the South after the Civil War; every responsible commentator who has tried to explain the rise of Huey Long has discussed the condition of the post-bellum South. Willie's personal indifference to money and his moral and intellectual isolation from his retainers clearly parallel Long's similar attitudes. Warren implies that Willie Stark's irrational attitude toward his son is caused in part by the deprivations of Stark's own youth (*AKM*, p. 244); at least one observer, Carleton Beals, thought that Long's attempt to make Louisiana State into the world's greatest university grew out of "a naive desire to experience a side of university life denied him in his youth."[41] And just as Huey publicly showed his concern for L. S. U. by his wild conduct at football games, his willingness to give state jobs to football players who made touchdowns and his interference with the coaching staff (his meddling caused Coach Biff Jones to resign), so Willie shows his concern for Tom Stark by his manic behavior at football games, his half-time promises not to forget the players and his willingness to override a coach's disciplinary

[40]Jackson (Miss.) *Clarion Ledger*, Sept. 11, 1935.

[41]Beals, *Story*, p. 205. Long's concern for *his* L. S. U. is remarkably like Stark's obsession with *his* charity hospital. Even Huey's stated belief that a university should be kept "absolutely clean and pure" sounds like Willie's plan to keep his hospital free from corruption. See "My University," *Time*, XXIV (Dec. 10, 1934), 43, and "Notes of the Seventeenth Annual Conference of the National Association of Deans and Advisors of Men, Feb. 29 — Mar. 2, 1935," pp. 44-48.

orders to win the championship. Even the fundamental question of Willie's sincerity, a problem central to the novel, was raised repeatedly about Long. When Anne Stanton asks Jack Burden if Willie means what he says, Jack can give her no answer because he wonders the same thing himself (*AKM*, p. 278). As Forrest Davis says, "The matter of Huey's sincerity remains the great riddle of the Delta."[42]

At the beginning of this essay I cited Warren's 1953 statement that although "it was the career of Long and the atmosphere of Louisiana that suggested the play that [became] the novel," *All the King's Men* is not a "biography of or apologia for" Huey Long; I also cited his 1963 statement that a mythical Long and metaphysical Louisiana gave him a line of thinking that he wrote about after the "factual world was only a memory, and therefore was ready to be absorbed freely into the act of imagination." What Warren seems to have absorbed, however, was most of Long's public career, including even minor details. And such words as "atmosphere," "myth" and "suggestion" do not seem adequate to describe the extent to which Warren, consciously or not, reproduced recognizable counterparts to people who actually associated with Long and endowed his fictional Boss with almost every one of the Kingfish's factual characteristics.

Or in different terms, Warren's statements are comparable to a claim that Shakespeare's Julius Caesar is neither a biography of nor an apologia for the historical Caesar but rather the result of a line of thinking suggested by Caesar's career and times. Such a claim would be true but would hardly reflect the degree to which Shakespeare relied on *The Lives of the Noble Greeks and Romans* for his material, North for his language and Plutarch for his interpretations. Or, an explanation that Shakespeare's characterization of Henry V is based on a legendary or mythical "Prince Hal" rather than on the real Henry of Lancaster because Shakespeare did not know the secret forces that motivated Henry would contain just as much truth and be just as misleading as Warren's explanation. Both writers have given us imaginative reworkings of historical materials. And if it be argued that Warren made obvious changes in what he knew to be literally true, Shakespeare's example should be a sufficient answer.

On the other hand, any suggestion that *All the King's Men* is any less a work of art because it owes so much to Huey Long is obviously as absurd as a similar charge would be against Shakespeare. For, as most readers know, the value of *All the King's Men* as a novel is not so much in the way people look and talk, the events that happen, or

[42]Davis, p. 4.

the things said, as in the meanings Jack Burden gives to all of these. It is one of the marks of Warren's genius that he used the career of Huey Long as the source of such a wealth of meanings without doing violence either to what is known about Long or to the integrity with which the meanings are worked out: indeed, that he was able to alter so little as he imposed the order of art on the chaos of actuality.

Cass Mastern and the
Awful Responsibility of Time

by Beekman W. Cottrell

It is an important fact about *All the King's Men* that the major philosophical image of the novel, the Spider Web, comes directly from the journal of Cass Mastern which, almost verbatim, forms the bulk of Chapter IV. This unit of the past pervades and profoundly influences the life of Jack Burden, whose search for definition as a man in the twentieth century is as important to the novel as the more immediately dominant history of Willie Stark. The story of Cass radiates through *All the King's Men*. It is only gradually that the reader comes to know how central it is as the source of Jack's salvation and as a testament that Warren, like Faulkner, sees the past as the arbiter of the present.

But first let us see how the story of Cass Mastern becomes a part of the novel at all. Warren has so planned the story that we meet the principals as they approach crises and learn of their past histories in a series of memory flashbacks, through the eyes and words of Jack, our narrator and guide. Thus events are not chronologically arranged, and areas of the past come forward as they are useful to Jack in the telling of his story. Once we know about Willie Stark and his rise to the governorship and have become aware of Jack's relationships, both spiritual and material, to the Boss, we are in a position to understand Burden's reluctance to dig up scandal from his friend Judge Irwin's past life. And yet to show us—the urge in Jack is both wryly sarcastic and proud—that he is a scholar with training in methods, perspective, and respect for the facts, Jack tells us about his first "excursion into the past"—and admits that it failed. We learn about Cass (a maternal uncle of Ellis Burden, the Scholarly Attorney), who lived during the Civil War and whose diaries and letters Jack

"Cass Mastern and the Awful Responsibility of Time" by Beekman W. Cottrell. From *All the King's Men: A Symposium*, edited by A. Fred Sochatoff and others (Pittsburgh: Carnegie Institute of Technology, 1957), Carnegie Series in English, no. 3, pp. 39-49. Reprinted by permission of the author and the publisher.

was using as the basis for a doctoral dissertation in American history. The Mastern papers tell about Cass' life from its beginnings, but their focus is on his college years, his secret love affair with the wife of his best friend, and his death in a wartime hospital. Scattered references to Mastern appear throughout *All the King's Men,* for Jack is continually aware of him, but as the novel progresses we learn why Jack first failed to complete his book, despite all the immediacy and intrinsic merit of Cass Mastern's life story as material for a dissertation.

The Jack Burden who undertook a Ph.D. and decided to deal with the Mastern papers was in no sense fully alive to his world. He was uncommitted and even unaware that some kind of commitment was either desirable or necessary. A major psychological proof of this lack of contact with reality was to be found in his periods of Great Sleep. These were the soft blocks of unreality wherein Jack could hide and dream and avoid both the facts of existence and the necessary job of interpreting them. He found out that he could master the facts easily enough, but he subconsciously refused to understand that there were truths inherent in them.

There were several ways, however, in which Jack was perfectly prepared for the task of writing Cass Mastern's life when he undertook it. The subject was, as he thought at the time, of familial concern; his love affair with Anne Stanton had come to an end because she saw that he had no goal, no direction, and little strength of character; and his work and aimless life as a newspaper reporter made the thought of settled study seem attractive. The prospect of an historical investigation, a neat job of recorded history, intrigued him, and the enterprise seemed fated once he had been sent the Mastern papers by a distant relative.

But Jack was not prepared to have the past take on greater reality than the present, nor was he prepared for a journal which began,

"I was born...in a log cabin in north Georgia, in circumstances of poverty, and if in later years I have lain soft and have supped from silver, may the Lord not let die in my heart the knowledge of frost and of coarse diet. For all men come naked into the world, and in prosperity 'man is prone to evil as the sparks fly upward.'" (p. 172)*

As Jack worked through the remarkable pages which followed, wrote up his notes, visited the house where Cass and Annabelle Trice had loved so passionately and so clandestinely and where her

*[Page references are to The Modern Library Edition of *All the King's Men,* 1953. —Ed.]

husband had shot himself after he learned of their affair, he came to
know very surely that this life, this history, was too strong for the
abilities of at least one historical researcher. What stopped Jack was
the fact that although Cass believed in love, he also believed in guilt
and responsibility — "my single act of sin and perfidy" (p. 189).

It was Jack's first confrontation with the most important philosophical theme of *All the King's Men:* "…if you could not accept the
past and its burden there was no future" (p. 461). Cass wrote,

> It was, instead, the fact that all of these things — the death of my friend,
> the betrayal of Phebe, the suffering and rage and great change of the
> woman I had loved — all had come from my single act of sin and per-
> fidy, as the boughs from the bole and the leaves from the bough. Or to
> figure the matter differently, it was as though the vibration set up in
> the whole fabric of the world by my act had spread infinitely and with
> ever increasing power and no man could know the end.   (p. 189)

At a considerable distance from his first contact with the idea, and
once again working on the life of Cass, Jack can rephrase and elaborate the second image, which conveys Warren's theme and reveals
Jack's own painfully developed philosophy of life.

> Cass Mastern lived for a few years and in that time he learned that the
> world is all of one piece. He learned that the world is like an enormous
> spider web and if you touch it, however lightly, at any point, the vibra-
> tion ripples to the remotest perimeter and the drowsy spider feels the
> tingle and is drowsy no more but springs out to fling the gossamer
> coils about you who have touched the web and then inject the black,
> numbing poison under your hide. It does not matter whether or not
> you meant to brush the web of things. Your happy foot or your gay
> wing may have brushed it ever so lightly, but what happens always
> happens and there is the spider, bearded black and with his great
> faceted eyes glittering like mirrors in the sun, or like God's eye, and
> the fangs dripping. (p. 200)

The Spider Web theory demands responsibility, and Jack only
gradually learns to become responsible. At first he simply put aside
the journals and boxed up the three-by-five cards. He moved, instead, toward his wife Lois, and into the oblivion of the Great Sleep.
But gradually the lesson Cass holds out from the vital past begins to
affect him; he comes to perceive the interresponsibility of things in
the world at large. What is most difficult for him to accept is the fact
that "it does not matter whether or not you meant to brush the web
of things." The revelation of his paternity, the loss of Judge Irwin

and Willie and Adam by circumstantial tragedy, and the realization that he himself had been a factor in driving Anne to Willie Stark— all these injections of the black and numbing poison finally lead Jack to an understanding of truth in the Spider Web sense.

Basically it was the *personal* sense of responsibility in Cass Mastern which Jack had at first been unable to accept or even recognize. Cass did not brush the Spider Web voluntarily. Chance threw him in with Annabelle Trice, and the vibrations of the web began. Their intense affair was wrong—sinful—in every way and Cass knew it. His sense of guilt came quickly and had far-reaching consequences. The suicide of Duncan Trice was the greatest personal confirmation for Cass that he was guilty of mortal sin and must atone. Close after it came Annabelle's revelation that she had sold the Negro slave Phebe down the Ohio River because "'...she was still staring at me, and her eyes were gold,...and bright and hard like gold. And I knew that she knew'" (p. 186). What Phebe knew was that Duncan had removed his golden wedding ring, for the first time since marriage, before the suicide and left it under his pillow as a mute testament to his knowledge of Annabelle's infidelity. She could not keep the ring, and gave it to Cass, who wore it always around his neck like a tiny albatross, to remind him of his sin. This indestructible evidence eventually comes, along with a photograph of Cass and the journals, to Jack Burden.

A hounding sense of guilt drove Cass to seek out Phebe, but in this he failed. After a quarrel of honor over the treatment of slaves, he lay gravely ill, willing death until he realized that such a wish was also a sin. Recovered, he prayed, read his Bible, prospered on the plantation, and freed his slaves. In so doing he extended his sense of personal responsibility from Phebe to all those in bondage. Still in an attempt to atone (but in addition, a convinced Abolitionist), Cass entered the Civil War as a private for the South though his brother Gilbert offered him a commission. He was determined to march with the men of his own heritage, and yet in his heart had decided not to use the rifle he carried even though it might save his life. Twice Cass met Jefferson Davis, the idealist whom practical, confident Gilbert Mastern ridiculed in these words, "'What we want now they've got into this is not a good man but a man who can win, and I am not interested in the luxury of Mr. Davis's conscience'" (p. 197). Cass, admiring Davis, reflected, "Mr. Davis was a good man. But the world is full of good men...and yet the world drives hard into darkness and the blindness of blood" (pp. 197-198). In Davis he saw a parallel for his own lonely choice. Both were committed to a course of action which they abhorred but which, as men aware of responsibility, they could not avoid.

Thus a love affair had progressively expanded to include the death of a friend, the question of enslavement, and finally, the engagement of a peaceful man in war. Cass Mastern had lost his life for a cause he could not in conscious support, and his journals dramatized the moral struggle for Jack Burden. Despite all its painfully acquired self-knowledge and the shift from personal guilt to collective responsibility, Cass' life seemed a failure to Jack. But the passionate convictions and the steps Cass took toward a responsible erasure of personal sin remained to be examined by an unmoored and drifting student of history. The lesson when first read was neither fully understood nor challenging enough to do anything but make Jack balk and run.

But Warren has seen to it that Cass' story will be understood, both by the reader and finally by Jack. It is unique in color, tone, and personal appeal; and the episode is effectively placed in *All the King's Men* so that its impact will be both intense and pervasive. In addition to the general first-person narrative, Warren offers another level, a yet more personal and vivid "I" in Cass Mastern, telling a story which is complete before the judgment of history. Further, the Mastern story has a sense of immediacy which stems from its very words, suddenly romantic, high-sounding, personal, and emotionally charged, and from a technique of direct quotation which invites participation in the drama. By means of Cass, Warren creates a past which brings both Jack and the reader up sharply. This past, so important to the philosophy of the novel, must seem valid, believable, and real. Both the shift in tone and Warren's mastery (again, like Faulkner's) of the Civil War period help to make the point.

To indicate their power, the events are told in a unit, as Jack learned them, and the reader then becomes aware how heavily this lump of history weights upon Jack's conscious and subconscious mind. Cass' story is told before we know all of the contemporary events of the novel and thus reinforces a major thesis: the interdependence of past and present. All of the major plot revelations follow the Mastern episode in the time scheme of the novel, and the author can build on the bulk of current time, the strong events it offers, and a growing involvement on the part of the reader as Jack gradually absorbs the lessons of Cass' life. Coming as it does into the grey life of Jack the student, half-alive and uncommitted to any course of action, the story of Cass Mastern is patently one of the few vivid aspects of his existence just then. His boyhood at Burden's Landing has taken on a dream-of-gold quality, there has been only a foretaste of Willie Stark's potential influence, and love has failed him. Cass Mastern's love affair with Annabelle stands for the kind of magnificent sexual fulfillment which he might have had with Anne. Thinking of the fateful frustration of a rainy evening, Jack comments dryly,

> So, I observed, my nobility (or whatever it was) had had in my world almost as dire a consequence as Cass Mastern's sin had had in his. Which may tell something about the two worlds. (p. 315)

Gradually, however, the worlds begin to join, as the events and decisions of Cass' life begin to pervade Jack's own. Neither the Great Sleep nor a complete change of occupation can dispel the haunting quality of Cass' words or the burning zeal in the eyes of the photograph. Since the maturing Jack is a man who thinks primarily in concrete images, his mind gradually seizes upon the vibrating web and works it into a very complete philosophical example. Thus the spider web as responsibility becomes for Jack a kind of opposite view to his earlier convictions, for which he also eventually finds an image in the Great Twitch, inspired by the hitchhiker he picks up on his drive east from California. Thoughts inspired by Cass are never far from Jack's mind. The image of a telegram—any telegram—half-shoved under any door, its contents unknown, brings to Jack's imagination the great all-seeing eye of the spider who looks "with his great faceted eyes glittering like mirrors in the sun, or like God's eye," watching the little man—any little man—who is caught in the web of unknown facts concealed within such a telegram. Jack loves to stop briefly in thought to generalize or sum up, and most often these generalizations are connected with Cass. Contrasting facts and truth he says, "So I walked out of a room, the room where the facts lived in a big box of three-by-five-inch note cards..." (p. 167), and carries the memory even further into the abstract with "...maybe you cannot ever really walk away from the things you want most to walk away from" (p. 48).

When Jack meets Willie he thinks of Cass' strong-willed brother, Gilbert, who was just as much a man of expedience and driving strength. He makes a parallel: "...perhaps the Gilbert Masterns are always at home in any world. As the Cass Masterns are never at home in any world" (p. 173). What Jack learned about Gilbert Mastern as compromiser and about Cass as idealist he applied to himself and to Adam Stanton. Much later, when he was able to see the life of

Mastern in perspective, he found parallels between Cass and himself, and contrasts between Annabelle and Anne Stanton. Later still, he thought of Trice and Cass as he pondered the love affair which Judge Irwin had carried on with his mother in the home of the Scholarly Attorney.

When Jack reads in the journals that Cass moved down the crowded road after his first Civil War battle "as in a dream" and felt that henceforward he would "live in that dream..." (p. 198), Jack thinks of his own dreamlike existence, a major segment of which followed his work with the Mastern papers. And after he has unearthed the scandal in Judge Irwin's life, consciously mindful of the slave Phebe's direct gaze which proclaimed full knowledge of Cass' sin, he writes with growing personal knowledge of the Spider Web: "And all times are one time, and all those dead in the past never lived before our definition gives them life, and out of the shadow their eyes implore us" (p. 242).

So much a part of him have the journals become that Jack even thinks of Cass when he is describing himself retrospectively as the boy Anne Stanton loved that summer by the bay:

> She was in love with a rather tall, somewhat gangly, slightly stooped youth of twenty-one, with a bony horse face, a big almost askew hook of a nose, dark unkempt hair, dark eyes (not burning and deep like the eyes of Cass Mastern, but frequently vague or veiled, bloodshot in the mornings, brightening only with excitement), big hands that worked and twisted slowly on his lap, plucking at each other, and twisted big feet that were inclined to shamble... (p. 299)

But in spite of a growing realization that he must accept the past, and a constantly changing knowledge of the past he must absorb and adjust to, Jack's own unreal idealism persists in a roundabout way. He is not strong enough to accept full responsibility, as Cass was. To delay the inevitable self-test, he fixes on Adam Stanton, an unswerving idealist. He reveals to Adam and Anne the collusion of Governor Stanton in the Judge Irwin affair. Actually, this is a kind of self-punishment for his own position of uneasy compromise with Willie, given perversely to those he loves. He is testing the idealism of the White Knight to the utmost, almost driving Adam toward murder or violence. It is a subconscious desire to have Adam— whose brand of purity Jack still feels may be an answer to compromise—act for him, even against Willie. In the end this does happen, although by then Jack has tried desperately to hide the facts and thus bank Adam's idealistic fires.

The truths for Jack in Cass Mastern's life become more persistently clear. Even in Willie, whose declarations once appeared so sure and so opposite to responsibility, Jack perceives glimpses of truth.

> Now I had a new question to ask him: If he believed that you had to make the good out of the bad because there wasn't anything else to make it out of, why did he stir up such a fuss about keeping Tiny's hands off the Willie Stark Hospital? (p. 278)

This, and that uncertain wink, and Willie's dying words—together they begin to mean that a hidden layer of value and responsibility now and again showed through the rough surface material of Willie Stark.

So at the end of the novel Jack can return to Burden's Landing, the symbol of his youth, to accept a new past from the eyes of his gallant mother and to resume work on the story of Cass Mastern. Referring to Judge Irwin's will he writes: "But I still had the money, and so I am spending it to live on while I write the book I began years ago, the life of Cass Mastern, whom once I could not understand but whom, perhaps, I now may come to understand" (p. 463). Life has truly been motion toward knowledge for him. This new past is the same one he had considered "tainted and horrible" until he could begin to realize the truth in Willie's belief that goodness can only come out of badness "because there isn't anything else to make it out of." Rejecting badness entirely results in the death of an Adam Stanton, the withdrawal of a Lucy Stark, the mental wandering of an Ellis Burden. Accepting badness and necessary compromise can also result in the loss of a Willie Stark, but it cannot blot out his greatness. Such greatness was due, Jack comes to believe, in large part to a sense of personal responsibility about life—a responsibility which finally linked Willie, Judge Irwin, Anne Stanton, Sadie Burke, and Jack's mother. Once Jack can realize these individuals as responsible beings, dealing with good and evil as the circumstances permit or direct, willing to accept the results of the Spider Web's vibrations, he is ripe to join their company. Anne can now see in him the maturity and potential strength she had found first in her father, then in Adam, then in Willie. Jack's mother can be reconciled to a responsible life after a sacrifice which has led her son to a compassionate understanding of her. Jack learns that all are equally balanced, equally vulnerable, on the infinite Spider Web of God.

Perhaps the hardest task of all for Jack in his new maturity is the acceptance of Ellis Burden. The care and consideration which he gives to the Scholarly Attorney surely confirm Anne's full faith in her husband. And the old man, in heightened awareness after a long, numbing hiatus, proclaims in a final clarity before death, "The creation of man whom God in his foreknowledge knew doomed to sin was the awful index of God's omnipotence" (p. 462). Jack adds, "I was not certain but that in my own way I did believe what he had said" (p. 463).

Cass Mastern's life, the Spider Web as it demands accountability of each man, and the dramatic events of the novel all proclaim that the patterns of life are tragic. It is for Jack to decide what his attitude will be in the face of the evidence. Events themselves help him to choose. Finally, as one after another of his beloved friends is lost, it becomes really only a decision to face squarely the "convulsion of the world."

In the particular context of *All the King's Men*—or, indeed, in the particular context of life—such a mature vision is not easily attained or made convincing. But both Jack and the reader must understand the hard-won philosophy. As a vital and valid testament from another epoch where such a struggle took place, the story of Cass is both relevant and persuasive. The Civil War, in which brother fought against brother, offers a well-known and appropriate framework for a parable from another time to reinforce the lesson of the present. Cass, for Jack at least a kind of Cassandra, proclaims that men must accept the burden of intolerance and strife. Ironically, as in the Trojan War, the message first falls on barren soil. Only after the wreck of lives close to Jack can he understand the prophecy which lay before him. Only in an aftermath of self-knowledge and sorrowful loss can he begin to understand what Cass meant when he wrote from his death-bed, "I do not question the Justice of God, that others have suffered for my sin, for it may be that only by the suffering of the innocent does God affirm that men are brothers..." (p. 199).

Cass wrote of his own brother, "perhaps only a man like my brother Gilbert can in the midst of evil retain enough of innocence and strength to bear their eyes upon him and to do a little justice in the terms of the great injustice" (pp. 195-196). Jack, having known Willie Stark and his struggle to make good out of bad, can at length proclaim, with Lucy, that such a battle is greatness. The words "justice *in the terms of* the great injustice" furnish the major clue for the mature Jack, for the revitalized Lucy, and for the reader who wishes to understand Warren's message aright.

With the help of Cass Mastern, Jack Burden learns the difficulty of coming to terms with the world, of achieving philosophical balance in any age. Cass, facing death in the wartime hospital (his final words to Gilbert were, "Remember me, but without grief. If one of us is lucky, it is I..."—p. 199), realized fully "the awful responsibility of time" as the arbiter of existence. Jack, profiting from both senses of the phrase, comes *in time* to realize this truth and to face his meaningful future in kinship with the past. If the earlier world seems more vivid than the present, this may tell us, as Jack suspects, something about the two worlds, and exemplify the terrible division of the greyer, flatter, and less creative age we live in, must understand, and must accept.

The Metaphysics of Demagoguery:
All the King's Men by Robert Penn Warren

by Jonathan Baumbach

History is blind but man is not.   ALL THE KING'S MEN

Although Robert Penn Warren is a generation or so older than, with one exception, any of the writers treated in this study, he is technically a post-Second-World-War novelist. That is, the larger body of his fiction, including his major novel *All the King's Men,* has been published since 1945. Though a valuable novelist, Warren is also notably a playwright, poet, teacher, scholar, and critic—a man of letters in the best sense. The problem is, how does a man write a novel unself-consciously, when he is aware just how the critic, created perhaps in his own image, is likely to read it? The answer is, he doesn't. At least Warren doesn't.

Almost all of Warren's fiction suffers somewhat from the determined this-marriage-can-be-saved compatibility between Warren the novelist and Warren the explicator. The harder he tries to fuse the two selves, the farther apart they spring, as if resistant to the meddling of an outsider. As Eric Bentley has actually observed, "The problem lies precisely in his [Warren's] being so two-sidedly gifted; he evidently finds it endlessly difficult to combine his two sorts of awareness." Warren's novels are informed by a fairly complex set of intellectual alternatives, while at the same time they rely for their movement on frenetically charged melodramatic action, often for its own sake, for the sake merely of narrative excitement. Though Warren is a serious novelist, and at his best a brilliant prose writer, there is a curious separation in his novels between the events of the narrative and the meaning Warren insists they accommodate.

"The Metaphysics of Demogoguery: *All the King's Men* by Robert Penn Warren." From Jonathan Baumbach, *The Landscape of Nightmare* (New York: New York University Press, 1965). 16-34. Reprinted by permission of the author and the publisher.

Of Warren's eight novels to date, *All the King's Men* (1946) seems to me the most achieved, the most serious and the most enduring — for all its flaws, one of our near-great novels. For some time *All the King's Men* was misread as a disturbingly sympathetic fictionalized account of the demagogic career of Huey Long. Approached as an historical document, the book was condemned by politically liberal critics as a florid, rhetorical justification for a Napoleonic brand of American neo-fascism. There is no need any longer to point out the irrelevancy of this attack, to explain that Jack Burden is the center of the novel and that Willie Stark, "the man of fact," is not *actually* Huey Long, but a kind of "Mistah Kurtz." In fact, in recent years a critical orthodoxy has clustered about Warren's novels, which is not unlike those contemporary angels headed by C. S. Lewis and Douglas Bush who guard the gates around Milton's *Paradise Lost,* protecting it from profanation by the infernal satanists. In both cases the defense is warranted; there is a real enemy. But in both cases the enemy is already within the gates. Though Warren intends Jack Burden to be the center of the novel, Willie Stark is by virtue of his energy the more realized and interesting character. Burden, as thinly disguised authorial spokesman, is a literary conception, created from other fiction rather than from life, a combination, if you can imagine it, of Nick Carraway and Sam Spade. Whatever Warren's intention, the character of Willie Stark, a colossus of human and inhuman possibilities, inadvertently dominates the novel. Inevitably, a distortion results, the kind of distortion which would permit *All the King's Men* to be read as the story of Willie Stark's rise and fall (a tragedy of over-reaching pride brought low by retributive justice).

For all that, Jack Burden, acquiescent narrator, at once vicarious Willie and vicarious Adam, is the novel's center, the ultimate synthesizer of its polarities. While Willie and Adam die unfulfilled, Jack completes the spiritual voyage; he moves, an exemplary sleepwalker, from sin to recognition and guilt to redemption and rebirth. Jack's ritual search for a true father, or at least a true absolute, leads him into Willie's employ (on the coat-tails of his political ascension). Ironically, there is a certain amount of narcissism in Jack's discipleship because he has, in part, created Willie the "Boss," catalyzed him from the raw materials of "Cousin Willie from the country." At the outset, Willie is an innocent, a do-gooder whose campaign speeches are scrupulously honest and drearily dull. Jack gives him his first taste of the apple:

Hell, make 'em cry, make 'em laugh, make 'em think you're God-Almighty. Or make 'em mad. Even mad at you. Just stir 'em up, it doesn't matter how or why, and they'll love you and come back for more. Pinch them in the soft place. They aren't alive, most of 'em haven't been alive in twenty years. Hell, their wives have lost their teeth and their shape, and likker won't set on their stomachs, and they don't believe in God, so it's up to you to give 'em something to stir 'em up and make 'em feel again.... But for Sweet Jesus' sake don't try to improve their minds.[1]

This is the first and last time that Jack gives Willie a short course in cynical wisdom.[2] Once having learned the lesson, Willie becomes the teacher, the authority on man's fallen nature. As Willie tells Jack later on in his (and Warren's) characteristic evangelical rhetoric: "'Man is conceived in sin and born in corruption and passeth from the stink of the didie to the stench of the shroud. There is always something'" (p. 157).

It is Jack, however, who has initiated Willie's conversion from the man of idea to the man of fact, from romanticism to pragmatism. By demonstrating to him that his start in politics was made possible by political corruption, Jack destroys Willie's sense of innocence, de-creates him into manhood. While Jack, who suffers chronically from paralysis of the will, converts Willie through abstract example, Willie converts the uncommitted Jack through practical demonstration. The "Boss" Willie is Jack as he would like to be, but only if he could watch himself being it. For all his admiration of action, Jack is essentially a spectator, an historian waiting for history to happen. Willie performs history for him, tests the efficacy of Jack's theories, while Jack with clinical dispassion sits on the sidelines taking notes. (Jack's role as spectator is defined symbolically in the scene in which he sits in the hospital amphi-theatre watching Adam Stanton perform a lobotomy.) As a dutiful son, Jack Burden participates in and even admires his father's ruthless pragmatism without sensing his own culpability. What you refuse to know can't hurt you, but, as Jack discovers, for only so long as you can remain blind. The longer you avoid self-knowledge, however, the more vulnerable you are to its intrusion.

Aside from Willie, Jack has two other fathers: a nominal one who he thinks is real and whom he has rejected (Ellis Burden) and a

[1]Robert Penn Warren, *All the King's Men* (New York: Harcourt, Brace & World, Inc. 1946), p. 72. All quotations are from this edition.

[2]Taken out of context, this passage could conceivably pass for one of Willie's own speeches.

real one whom he admires and inadvertently kills (Judge Irwin). When Willie assigns him to get "something on" Judge Irwin, who has been outspoken in his criticism of Stark's administration, Jack is forced for the first time to choose between the prerogatives of opposing fathers. (Though he doesn't know that Irwin is his natural father, he respects, resents, and feels obligated to Irwin as a son to a father because of Irwin's decency and friendship over the years.) Looking for a way out of his predicament, Jack tells Willie that Irwin is "washed in the blood" and that an investigation of Irwin's past will be a waste of time. Willie knows, however, that man is fallen, that "there is always something." In investigating the facts of Irwin's life, Jack puts to the test the last illusion he has permitted himself to retain, that despite the rank and malodorous corruption which underlies so much of contemporary life, a truly good man like Irwin remains incorruptible. Jack has another naive notion which justifies the political dirt-digging he does so that Willie can blackmail his opponents: that the truth, regardless of its immediate effects, is always salutary and that unadulterated fact constitutes truth.

In search of the hidden facts of his real father's past, Jack visits Ellis Burden, the Scholarly Attorney turned Religious fanatic, his nominal father. It is here that the divergent influences of his trinity of fathers come into focus and are symbolically defined. Once again, Jack rejects the Scholarly Attorney, the weak saint, whose life of squalor, piety, and undiscriminating compassion seems purposeless to him when contrasted with Willie Stark's vigorous usefulness. This dispossessed nominal father has adopted a substitute son, George, a former circus aerialist who has reverted to childhood. George, redeemed through trauma into helpless innocence, spends his time making angels from masticated bread crusts. He is, in an ironic sense, Jack's brother. George's idiot purity embarrasses Jack and he rejects the image of his opposite (his innocent brother) along with his Scholarly Attorney father, along with the past. But, at the same time, he is again rejected by his father, who refuses to answer his questions about Irwin—who is unable to hear him when Jack calls him "Father." The visit is a failure; Jack learns nothing about Irwin, and he experiences the loss of his father all over again.

The uncovering of Irwin's one dishonorable act has massive, unaccountable ramifications. In consequence of Jack's discovery, Judge Irwin commits suicide. Anne Stanton has a self-destructive affair with Willie Stark, Adam Stanton kills Willie Stark, and Willie Stark's bodyguard kills Adam Stanton. For all his disinterested intentions, Jack must bear the burden of responsibility for this proliferation of tragedy. He has set it in motion as surely and perfectly as if he had consciously planned it. The "facts" that incriminate the Judge also indicate the complicity of Governor Stanton, who deliberately covered up for his friend. This further discovery destroys for both Anne and Adam Stanton the idealized notion of their father that has sustained them in their myth of purity as children of innocence—descendants of innocence. When Anne discovers that the purity of the old governor is tainted, she is able to shed her restrictive moral restraints as a snake sheds its skin. If there is no pure God, a pure Satan is the next best thing—he is at least whole. With the loss of her good father, Anne commits a sort of symbolic incest with the bad father—the new governor—searching for an absolute to replace the one she had lost. The loss of innocence in the novel for Jack, Willie, Anne, and Adam is concomitant with the loss of the good father.

It is Adam, Jack's innocent self, the least convincing of all Warren's characters, who guilelessly gives Jack his first lead in uncovering Irwin's blemished past. Adam answers Jack's cunning, direct question, "Was Judge Irwin ever broke?" because he is too ingenuous not to. However, Adam's innocent volunteering of harmless information about Judge Irwin is, in its effects, irresponsible as only innocence can be. It gives Jack the necessary clue to unearth Irwin's guilty secret, which, in ramification, destroys each of the participants in the central action of the novel. Adam's ingenuousness here anticipates his later, more destructive, act of innocence—his self-righteous assassination of Willie Stark. To say any more about Adam is beside the point. Whereas some of Warren's characters are half-human, half-idea, Adam is pure idea; he is an allegorical personification of *Innocence*. But without life, he is finally nothing, a figment of the author's imagination.

All of Warren's main characters experience at one time or another the loss of innocence and are characterized in terms of their accommodation to their Fall. Judge Irwin, sustained like Adam by the myth of self-purity, has attempted to evade the implications of his one intentionally corrupt act (his Fall) by shutting it out of his memory. Some thirty years later, Jack, the unacknowledged child of his loins, confronts him with the forgotten past. Jack's confrontation has a twofold significance; Jack is the manifestation of Irwin's other sin, his adulterous affair with Jack's mother, so that he becomes for Irwin the symbol of his fallen past, the tale-bearer of one crime and the embodiment of the other. Warren images Jack's information as a barb finding meat, suggesting its lethal nature. The Judge, illuminated by self-knowledge at once destructive and redemptive, bears his pain stoically. For a moment Irwin is tempted to reveal to his son the nature of their relationship in order that Jack withhold his information, but he doesn't—because it is beside the point.

> "I wouldn't hurt you," he said. Then, reflectively, added, "But I could stop you."
>
> "By stopping MacMurfee," I said.
>
> "A lot easier than that."
>
> "How?"
>
> "A lot easier than that," he repeated.
>
> "How?"
>
> "I could just..." he began, "I could just say to you—I could just tell you something....." He stopped then suddenly rose to his feet, spilling the papers off his knees. "But I won't," he said cheerfully and smiled directly at me. (p. 347)

The moment of recognition is averted. By not telling Jack—an act of mortal restraint—Irwin accepts full responsibility for his sin. Irwin's withholding of his "truth" is, given the occasion, more honorable than Jack's revelation of his. The next morning Jack is awakened by his mother's "bright, beautiful silvery soprano screams." In her hysteria, she continues to shriek at Jack, "You killed him. You killed him," without identifying the "him": "'Killed who?' I demanded, shaking her. 'Your father,' she said, 'your father and oh! you killed him'" (p. 350).

Without further clarification, Jack realizes what has happened as if he had known all the time, in the secret wisdom of instinct, that Irwin was his father. That the Judge shoots himself through the heart indicates symbolically the implication of Jack's betrayal. Despite the terrible consequences of his act, Jack reflects on his responsibility for Irwin's suicide, as if it were an intellectual abstraction which does not touch him personally. At first he considers his father's death as the just retribution of Mortimer Littlepaugh, the man whom Irwin's own corrupt act drove to suicide. Then:

> Or had it been Mortimer? Perhaps I had done it. That was one way of looking at it. I turned that over and speculated upon my responsibility. It would be quite possible to say that I had none, no more than Mortimer had. Mortimer had killed Judge Irwin because Judge Irwin had killed him and I killed Judge Irwin because Judge Irwin had created me, and looking at matters in that light one could say that

Mortimer and I were only the twin instruments of Irwin's protracted and ineluctable self-destruction. For either killing or creating may be a crime punishable by death, and the death always comes by the criminal's own hand and every man is a suicide. If a man knew how to live he would never die.   (p. 353)

It is a characteristically easy rationalization for Jack, one which enables him to avoid for a time the implications of his behavior. Like every man, he too is a suicide (though a moral rather than a physical one) and, ultimately, ineluctably, his sins revisit him like retributive ghosts. As a result of Irwin's death, Jack loses two fathers, the weak but saintly Scholarly Attorney and the strong but tainted judge. Willie Stark, the evil father, the father who has cuckolded him, is all that is left for Jack in a world of decimated fathers, and finally Jack kills him too. As Jack tells us, "'I had dug up the truth and the truth always kills the father.'" In a symbolic sense, only after Jack destroys his fathers can he become a man himself. As part of his quest for knowledge (manhood), Jack kills the fathers of his world only to resurrect them finally in himself.

Jack's articulated intellection dissipates the effect of this scene as it does much of the richly rendered experience of the novel. Granted his cleverness, Jack is verbally aware of too much, and also too little; Warren is forever peeking over his shoulder, but withholding from his narrator the whole picture. That Jack as narrator is almost always the deception of an insight ahead of the reader is one of the recurring distractions of the novel. With rare exception, the reader is not permitted to discover meanings; they are discovered for him.

When Willie loses his innocence, he is transformed almost overnight from the son of his world to its father. Willie's spiritual metamorphosis (which resembles Kurtz's in *Heart of Darkness*), though thematically subordinate to Jack's guilt-and-redemption passage, dominates the action of the novel. Willie's career anticipates and parallels Jack's, as a father's anticipates a son's, though it is enlarged where Jack's is diminished, and Willie never successfully makes the spiritual voyage back from hell. Like Kurtz, the "Boss" has gone too far into darkness ever to return into light.

Willie becomes governor. Ostensibly, his ends have not changed, only his means of achieving them. Gradually, however, the ends become inseparable from their means and Willie yields himself to his most voracious interior devils. The thesis is classic and bromidic: power tends to corrupt; absolute power tends to corrupt absolutely.

With a difference, however: Warren inverts the cliché; for all his sins, "Willie is a great man." This is the verdict of his wife Lucy, to whom he has been unfaithful, whose son he has destroyed through vanity, and of Jack Burden, whom he has disillusioned and nearly destroyed. Since the redeemed Jack Burden, who has moved from blindness to whole sight represents, one must believe, the point of view of the novel, this must stand as Warren's judgment of Stark. The question remains: Is it a reasonable judgment borne out by the experience of the novel? Or is it a piece of gratuitous iconoclasm, the cliché-anti-cliché?

Warren enlists sympathy for Willie by indicating that the context in which he is forced to operate (southern politics) is unreclaimably corrupt. Whereas Tiny Duffy and Willie's opponent MacMurfee are interested in petty graft as an end, Willie's ego wants nothing less than recognition by posterity. Willie is a real devil at sup among dwarfed, flabby devils; in that he is more real and more potent than the others, he is to that extent more admirable. Once Willie has fallen, he discovers his true voice, the voice of the rabble rouser, the appeal to primordial violence:

> You asked me what my program is. Here it is, you hicks. And don't you forget it. Nail 'em up! Nail up Joe Harrison. Nail up anybody who stands in your way. Nail up MacMurfee if he don't deliver. You hand me the hammer and I'll do it with my own hand. Nail 'em up on the barn door. (p. 96)

The easier it becomes for Willie to manipulate the crowd, the less respect he has for its common fallen humanity. As he becomes more powerful, he becomes, like Kurtz and like Macbeth, more voracious, more proud, more evil. Willie's palpable moral decline is manifested for us when he covers up for an underling who has taken graft. It is not in the act of covering up but in his justification for it that Willie's inhumanity and presumption are manifested:

> My God, you talk like Byram was human! He's a thing! You don't prosecute an adding machine if a spring goes bust and makes a mistake. You fix it. Well, I fixed Byram. I fixed Byram. I fixed him so his unborn great-grandchildren will wet their pants on this anniversary and not know why. Boy, it will be the shock in the genes. Hell, Byram is just something you use, and he'll sure be useful from now on.
> (p. 136)

Willie's self-defining presumption is that he *knows* himself a superior being, aspiring to law, to omnipotence, to God. The ma-

chine metaphor he employs reveals his attitude not only toward
Byram but toward the populace in general: people are things to
be used by him, "the Boss," for *his* purposes. From Willie's "bulging-
eyed" point-of-view, everything, all existence, has been set in motion
to serve him.

Willie's will to power, his lust for omnipotence, is defeated by
what might be called a tragic virtue. Despite Willie's professed thesis
that "you have to make the good out of the bad because that's all you
have to make it out of," that all men are innately corrupt, that
"political graft is the grease that keeps the wheels from squeaking,"
he wants to build a magnificent, immaculate hospital as his gift to
the state, untainted by the usual petty corruption and graft. In pursuing this ideal, Willie refuses a deal with Gummy Larson, the
power behind his enemy MacMurfee, whose defection to Willie
would leave the "Boss" all but unopposed. Having fallen from
Paradise into Hell, Willie wishes—his one romantic illusion—to
regain his lost purity, to buy back Paradise. Willie tries to explain
his motives to Jack:

> "Can't you understand either? I'm building that place, the best in the
> country, the best in the world, and a bugger like Tiny is not going to
> mess with it, and I'm going to call it the Willie Stark Hospital and it
> will be there a long time after I'm dead and gone and you are dead
> and gone and all those sons-of-bitches are dead and gone and anybody,
> no matter he hasn't got a dime, can go there..."
>
> "And will vote for you," I said.
>
> "I'll be dead," he said, "and you'll be dead, and I don't care whether
> he votes for me or not, he can go there and..."
>
> "And bless your name," I said.

That Willie, so compellingly articulate on other occasions, cannot
cogently rationalize his motives suggests that they are contradictory
to him as well as to Jack. He wants at once to be noble and to have
everyone admire his nobility—selflessness for the sake of self. Yet,
and herein lies the contradiction, he also wants redemption.

As part of his obsessive desire to transcend his corruption, his
dream of greatness, Willie hires Adam Stanton to run his hospital,
hoping through connection, through transfusion of spirit, to inform himself with Adam's innocence. Ironically, Willie has, with
almost perfect instinct, chosen his redeemer, his redeemer as executioner. Adam and Willie as ideological polarities must inevitably
merge or destroy each other. Jack unites them, he is the means of
their collaborative self-destruction.

Willie's brief affair with Adam's sister Anne, is another extension of his specious quest for innocence. What Willie pursues is not innocence, really, but seeming innocence—respectability. His holy search for the false grail is the tragic flaw in his otherwise perfect expediency. Willie's lost innocence resides not with Adam and Anne, but with his wife Lucy and his father; his substitution of Anne for Lucy symbolizes his degeneration, his spiritual blindness. In his obsession with purity, Willie makes an enemy of the spiteful Tiny Duffy and puts too much faith in the erratically naive, the fallen innocent, Adam, thereby predicating his own destruction. Duffy makes an anonymous phone call to Adam, falsifying the implications of Anne's affair with Willie. The inflexibly idealistic Adam, unable to live in an imperfect world, acts as the unwitting tool of vengeful petty corruption and gratuitously murders Willie. Specious innocence and cowardly corruption conspire to destroy the "Boss" at the height of his power and at the threshold of his apparent self-reform.

Willie's deathbed scene is the most potent of the various dramatic climaxes in the novel. In it Warren brings sharply into focus the moral paradox of Willie's ethic—the tragedy of his unachieved, over-reaching ambition; it is rendered as Judge Irwin's death is not, as a profoundly affecting experience. It is the death of Jack's last symbolic father—in extension of all his fathers—leaving him, for a time, alone and uncommitted in the chaos of his ungoverned universe. I quote the scene at length because it is a resonant fusion of idea and action, a moment of illumined truth.[3]

> For a minute he didn't speak but his eyes looked up at me, with the light still flickering in them. Then he spoke: "Why did he do it to me?"
>
> "Oh, God damn it," I burst out, very loud, "I don't know." The nurse looked warningly at me.
>
> "I never did anything to him," he said.
>
> "No, you never did."
>
> He was silent again, and the flicker went down in his eyes. Then, "He was all right, the Doc."
>
> I nodded.
>
> I waited, but it began to seem that he wasn't going to say any more. His eyes were on the ceiling and I could scarcely tell that he was breathing. Finally, the eyes turned toward me again, very slowly, and I

---

[3]I would like to believe that the truth of a serious work of art is a partial illumination of an ultimately incomprehensible mystery. When the truths of a novel are too conclusive, they are often not truths at all but, at best, popular accommodations.

almost thought that I could hear the tiny painful creak of the balls in
their sockets. But the light flickered up again. He said, "It might have
been all different, Jack."

I nodded again.

He roused himself more. He even seemed to be straining to lift his
head from the pillow. "You got to believe that," he said hoarsely.

The nurse stepped forward and looked significantly at me.

"Yes," I said to the man on the bed.

"You got to," he said again. "You got to believe that."

"All right."

He looked at me, and for a moment it was the old strong, probing, demanding glance. But when the words came this time, they were very
weak. "And it might have been different yet," he whispered. "If it
hadn't happened, it might—have been different—even yet."   (p. 400)

Willie's deathbed claim is an easy one to make; it is as impossible to
prove as to disprove. One is tempted to say to him, as Jake does to
Brett at the end of *The Sun Also Rises,* "Isn't it pretty to think so?"
though significantly Jack does not. However, it is not out of motives
of sentiment that Jack withholds his ironic disbelief. He is not fully
convinced that Willie's self-justification is unjust. The possibility
remains: "It might have been different—even yet." Willie is, after
all, a paradox.

In becoming Willie's executioner, Adam, in his blind way, follows
the example of Willie's career—he becomes Willie. For the "man of
fact" and the "man of idea," as Jack classified them, there has been
an alternation of roles. Each incomplete, seeking completeness, has
chosen his polar opposite as an exemplary image. In building the
hospital without the "grease" of political graft, Willie is operating
idealistically—in Adam's image. In brutally shooting down Willie,
Adam is acting as disciple of the man whose power-authority is
symbolized by the meat axe. From Jack's standpoint, Willie is superior to Adam: "A man's virtue may be but the defect of his desire, as
his crime may be but a function of his virtue." If a man has not faced
temptation, or, as in Adam's case, has not admitted its existence, his
purity is illusory and beside the point.

Willie's relationship to his son Tom is another variation on the
novel's father-son conflict, and it serves as an ironic comment both
on Jack's relationship to his real father and to Willie. Jack's search
into Irwin's discreditable past is continually juxtaposed to scenes of
Willie worshipfully watching Tom perform on the football field:

"'He's my boy—and there's not any like him—he'll be All-American....'" Tom Stark is the perfect physical extension of Willie's wishful self-image; he is all man of action—with the bottle, on the gridiron, and in bed—one hundred percent performance, no waste. Burden sees him as "one hundred and eighty pounds of split-second, hair trigger, Swiss-watch beautiful mechanism." Inhuman but perfect, he is the embodiment of Willie's crass values. Willie is willing to overlook Tom's personal decay so long as he continues to function as a perfect mechanism on the football field and so sate Willie's rapacious vanity. Willie's attitude toward Tom is symbolic of his attitude toward the governmental machine—proud, permissive, and blind. Corruption is permissible because it "keeps the wheels from squeaking." His failure with Tom is, symptomatic of his potential failure as governor; to satisfy his vanity Willie would have all men, even his own son, made into functioning "things." Inadvertently, Willie destroys Tom, who is, outside of personal power, the "thing" he loves most in his world. When Tom has been barred from playing football for breaking college rules (the boy manages, among his heroics, to cripple one girl in an auto crash and to impregnate another), Willie pressures the coach into reinstating him. Almost immediately after Tom comes into the game, as if in direct consequence of Willie's corrupt use of authority, his spine is snapped by a vicious tackle. As a result, the son of the man-of-action is left actionless, without the use of his arms and legs. As the emotional paralysis of Jack catalyzes, in a sense, the action of Willie, Willie's action causes the physical paralysis of Tom. The irony is evident: ultimately a machine stops, even a perfect Swiss-made mechanism breaks down if it is dropped too often. The sins of the father are visited on the son. Similarly, the "breaking" of the son anticipates the destruction of the father; it is an intimation of Willie's mortality.

Whereas in Jack's case the son kills the father, in Willie's the father kills the son. However, Tom is, through the ineluctable chain of cause and effect, also the instrument of Willie's destruction. As a consequence of Tom's impregnating the daughter of one of MacMurfee's men, Willie is forced through blackmail to compromise his principles and give the corrupt Gummy Larson the hospital-construction contract. After Tom's injury, however, the guilt-ridden Willie breaks the contract. Tiny Duffy, who has been intermediary in the deal, exacts his vengence; he initiates Willie's murder through Adam's pride.

Before Adam shoots him down, Willie accepts Tom's paralysis as a judgment for his sins and seeks expiation through good works:

"you got to start somewhere." As Irwin ultimately redeems Jack, Tom almost redeems Willie, but not quite; after his fall, Humpty-Dumpty cannot be put together again. Willie, like Tom's paralyzed body, is denied rebirth. Willie's death does, however, make possible the redemption of Tom's illegitimate son, whom Lucy decides to adopt and name, of all names, Willie Stark. Through his son's son, Willie regains his lost innocence.

With the death of Willie, the effective father, Jack has no one left to whom he can transfer his responsibility. However, before he can achieve manhood, Jack has one other father with whom he has to come to terms—Cass Mastern; the subject of his Ph.D. dissertation is Jack's historic father. The episode of Cass Mastern, a self-contained short story with the novel, is intended as a gloss (in Warren's term, "the myth") on the larger action of the main narrative. Though it illuminates certain themes in *All the King's Men* and is in itself an exceptionally resonant tale, Cass's tragedy is hardly indispensable to the novel. In any event, at the cost of temporarily stopping the action, it gives added dimension to Burden's odyssey into self-knowledge, his passage from innocence to limbo to guilt to redemption. Though Jack has pieced together all the facts of Cass Mastern's life, he is unable to complete his dissertation. The significance of Cass's story eludes him, though he is aware that it has significance. Neither Jack's early philosophic idealism ("What you don't know won't hurt you") nor his disillusioned belief in the Great Twitch (that man is an involuntary mechanism and no one is responsible for anything) is adequate to a comprehension of Cass's sainthood. Cass, though innocent and virtuous, falls into an affair with Annabelle Trice, his best friend's wife. As a consequence, three lives are destroyed. Thereafter Cass, suffused with guilt, makes his existence a continuous penance for his sin. He finally joins the southern army and gives up his life while refusing to fire a shot in his own defense. Through martydom he achieves expiation. At the end, Cass becomes a religious fanatic, and on his deathbed he sends a strange letter to his successful brother. The passage is typical of the evangelical eloquence of Warren's rhetoric:

> Remember me, but without grief. If one of us is lucky, it is I. I shall have rest and I hope in the mercy of the Everlasting and his blessed election. But you, my dear brother, are condemned to eat bread in bitterness and build on the place where the charred embers and ashes are and to make bricks without straw and to suffer in the ruin and guilt of our dear Land and in the common guilt of man.   (p. 162)

Cass's martyrdom is exemplary; it is not only his own guilt for which he has suffered and died but the guilt of the land, "the common guilt of man." In the mystery of Cass's life and death resides the meaning of Jack's life, which is to say the essential meaning of all our lives. As Cass has written in his journal, and as Jack finally discovers for himself, "'It is a human defect—to try to know oneself by the self of another. One can only know oneself in God and His great eye.'" After the recognition of his guilt, it is in God that Cass does find himself; similarly, after Jack accepts his guilt, it is in himself that he finds Cass and, ultimately, God. The recognition of guilt for Cass (and by implication for Jack) is an awesome discovery.

> It was, instead, the fact of all these things—the death of my friend, the betrayal of Phebe, the suffering and rage and great change of the woman I had loved—all had come from my single act of sin and perfidy, as the boughs from the bole and the leaves from the bough. Or to figure the matter differently, it was as though the vibration set up in the whole fabric of the world by my act had spread infinitely and with ever increasing power and no man could know the end. I did not put it into words in such fashion, but I stood there shaken by a tempest of feeling.   (p. 178)

Cass's revelation is existential; that is, since the ramifications of a particular act are for the most part unknowable and the inherent responsibility for its entire chain reaction inescapable, the burden of guilt is endless—and unbearable. So Cass, in search of redemption, tracks down the various consequences of his act of sin only to discover that there is no undoing of the harm he has already caused. What he has done is irrevocable. It is only by "living in God's eye"— a saint's life—that he can hope to achieve expiation and redemption.

Since Duncan Trice, who is considerably older than Cass, initiates him into vice, he is, in effect, the father of Cass's adultery with Annabelle. What Cass has learned from Duncan he had put into practice with Duncan's wife. Therefore, Cass's crime, Warren suggests, is implicitly incestuous, for if Duncan, the man whose death he effects, is his "substitute" father, Annabelle as his wife is a sort of symbolic mother. This is essentially what Cass understands when he proclaims himself "'the chief of sinners and a plague spot on the body of the human world.'"

Cass's experience acts as an anticipatory parallel to Jack's own nightmare passage, though the connections are remote and abstract. When Jack discovers that Duffy "had killed Stark as surely as though his own hand had held the revolver," he feels absolved of responsibility, free at last to act, to vindicate the deaths of Willie and Adam However, Jack's newborn sense of freedom is illusory. It is for him another evasion of responsibility, in a way the least admirable of all. Convincing himself as Willie had, and as Adam had when he squeezed the trigger, that an act is a self-willed moral entity, Jack assumes for himself the role of avenging angel; he wishes to destroy Duffy in order to justify himself. However, after Jack chastises Duffy, "'You are the stinkingest louse God ever let live!'" and threatens him with exposure, he realizes that "'I had tried to make Duffy into a scapegoat for me and to set myself off from Duffy,'" that Duffy is his alter ego, his corrupt brother, and that whatever he had said about Duffy was also true of himself. In the power of Warren's prose, we get the visceral horror of Jack's self-revulsion:

> It was as though in the midst of the scene Tiny Duffy had slowly and like a brother winked at me with his oyster eye and I had known he knew some nightmare truth, which was that we were twins bound together more intimately and disastrously than the poor freaks of the midway who are bound by the common stitch of flesh and gristle and the seepage of blood. We are bound together forever and I could never hate him without hating myself or love myself without loving him.
>
> And I heaved and writhed like the ox or the cat, and the acid burned my gullet and that's all there was to it and I hated everybody and myself and Tiny Duffy and Willie Stark and Adam Stanton.   (p. 417)

Jack, by evading the responsibility for his own sins, had amid the corruption about him, retained the illusion of innocence. Since he had not acted out of conscious choice, but had merely yielded to the demands of the "Boss," he had been able to slough off the burden of guilt. Once he discovers himself free to act, he becomes aware that the possibility of all acts, the whole spectrum of good and evil, are in him; that he is, as human being, Oedipus and Duffy and Willie and everyone else. Having discovered the magnitude of his guilt — that he is responsible not only for his own sins but for all sins — Jack begins his return from the interior hell in which he has languished so long. He cannot leave hell, of course, until he has discovered its boundaries.

When Jack runs into "Sugar-Boy," Willie's driver and bodyguard (*the* man of action), he is presented with the opportunity of destroying Duffy with no risk to himself. He restrains himself not out of the paralysis ("the defect of desire") which prevented him many years before from making love to Anne when she offered herself to him but because Duffy is his "twin," and if he can sanction Duffy's murder he must sanction his own. (Cass refused to kill in the Civil War because: "'How can I, who have taken the life of my friend, take the life of an enemy, for I have used up my right to blood?'") Jack's refusal to take easy vengeance on Duffy is not inaction but a decisive moral act.

For a time, as a projection of his self-hate, Jack has a baleful view of all humanity. When he comes to love his mother, whom he has rejected long ago, he is able as a consequence to stop hating himself, which also means no longer hating the rest of the world. The redemption of his mother through the recognition of her love for Irwin (his real father) is Jack's salvation; it reestablishes for him the existential possibility of love. However, as Jack discovers, the process has been circular, for "'by killing my father I have saved my mother's soul.'" This discovery leads Jack into a further revelation (which is Warren's thesis) that "'all knowledge that is worth anything is maybe paid for by blood.'"

For all his belief in the purgative powers of knowledge, Jack lies to his mother when she asks about the motives for Irwin's suicide, telling her that his father killed himself because of failing health. It is, however, a salutary lie, the least he can do for his mother. As his mother's rebirth has resurrected him, Jack's lie resurrects the image of his father for his mother. (Jack's withholding of the truth from his mother closely parallels Marlowe's lie to Kurtz's intended at the end of *Heart of Darkness.* In both cases the lie is noble, and, in a sense, the truth.) His reconciliation with his mother begins his reconciliation with the past. For without the past Jack cannot really participate in the world of the present. By rediscovering the past he is able to recreate the present, to be spiritually reborn into a world in which before his destructive self-awareness he had only acquiescently participated. He moves into his father's house, affirming his linear heritage, accepting for himself at last the role of man and father. He marries his boyhood sweetheart Anne Stanton, to whom he had once in love and innocence committed his life irrevocably. In marrying Anne, Jack saves her in much the same way Pip saves Estella at the end of *Great Expectations.* Anne is the symbol to him of his lost innocence, and in redeeming her he at last redeems himself. Having accepted the past with its hate and love, its guilt and pride, its evil and good, Jack can be regenerated into the world of the present, redeemed through suffering and self-knowledge.

When Stark and Adam destroy each other, Jack emerges from the vicarious experience of their deaths as the synthesis of their alternatives, as a whole man. Through the responsibility his manhood imposes on him, he brings the Scholarly Attorney, old and dying, into his home. Finally, it is the old man, the religious fanatic, the "unreal" father from whom Jack learns the ultimate facts of life, who becomes a "real" father. ("Each of us is the son of a million fathers.") Jack comes to believe in the old man's religious doctrine that "'The creation of evil is...the index of God's glory and His power. That had to be so that the creation of good might be the index of man's glory and power. But by God's help. By His help and in His wisdom'" (p. 437).

Through his "father," Jack is able to understand the significance of Cass Mastern's life in the "eye of God." After Jack's nominal father dies and he has completed his study of Cass Mastern, fulfilling at last all of his obligations to the past, he can leave Judge Irwin's house, the womb of his rebirth, and "go into the convulsion of the world, out of history into history and the awful responsibility of time." While Cass has sacrificed his life to redeem himself, Jack achieves redemption somewhat easily and painlessly. For this reason, Jack's ultimate salvation seems externally imposed (redemption as happy ending), abstract and literary rather than real. Yet to object to Warren's fine novel because it falls short of its potentialities seems finally presumption. To have it better than it is would be at the expense of gambling with what it has already achieved — a fool's risk. *All the King's Men* is a great scarred bear of a book whose faults and virtues determine one another. The greatness of this bear devolves upon the magnificence of its faults and the transcendence into art of its palpable mortality.

Right On!
All the King's Men
in the Classroom

by Earl Wilcox

The wide range of critical approaches given to Robert Penn Warren's *All the King's Men* suggests that this novel is his most provocative piece of writing. Between two and three dozen articles is a conservative count of the more important essays. Perhaps, as with all successful artistic endeavors, this novel has prompted comment of such diverse variety because it seems to have a bit of everything for everyone. I think this proliferation of commentary indicates a popularity which stems, in large part, from the reception the book has received in the college and university classroom.

As almost everyone knows, Warren's is a hallowed name in some literary circles because of his co-editing and authoring several anthologies, collections of essays, rhetoric texts, and of course because of his role in expanding New Criticism. But Warren alone of the now unfashionable New Critics has succeeded as a poet, novelist, critic, editor, essayist, and as a teacher. It is fitting, then, to emphasize that one sound reason for the continuing popularity and discussion of *All the King's Men* is that it is eminently teachable. *All the King's Men* has for more than twenty years been the subject of countless discussions in the college and university classrooms and corridors. And I assume that a salient reason for this appeal lies exactly in the complex nature of the novel itself. In particular the novel insists on literary, historical, psychological, sociological, philosophical relevance. Its tone is at once satiric and humorous; its mode is both realism and tragedy. Its style, themes, and characters continue to excite both students and teachers alike.

"Right On! *All the King's Men* in the Classroom" by Earl Wilcox. From *Four Quarters* 21 no. 4 (May, 1972), 69-78. Reprinted by permission of the author and LaSalle College.

All the King's Men is most teachable as a piece of fiction primarily because it *is* fiction before it is a tract for dictators or a thinly-veiled biography of Huey Long. (But I do not mean that the novel does not accommodate itself well to all these and other approaches simultaneously: indeed I think that it does accommodate itself to a multiplicity of approaches.) No one has yet claimed that this novel is the mythical "great American novel" which every writer is said to be trying to write; but the novel does have literary excellence on several levels.

There is, for example, the narrator, Jack Burden. Burden is one of our finest literary creations; he is "one of us," as Hemingway's Brett Ashley would say. And, as his name signifies, Burden is a modern Everyman, an Oedipus, a naif for whom things fall apart and who tries to put them back together again. Jack is a man imbued with the kind of personality which strikes terror in the hearts of all who recognize his dilemma. For the student searching for a fictional contemporary that he can dig and who tries to cope, Jack Burden suits well. And in a formal study in the classroom, Burden's counterpart is translatable and recognizable from everywhere. Here once again is Huck Finn or Holden Caulfield or Telemachus in search of a father. Here is the romantic Don Quixote, trying for the longest while to see the world as it ought to be and not as it is. Or Hamlet, who vacillates between being and not-being. The list is long and the spectrum wide in the arena of literary antecedents upon whom the teacher and student calls for useful, insightful comparison. Since some fiction courses seem to organize around comparisons and contrasts, and such courses often proceed chronologically, identifying these literary predecessors is a helpful beginning device.

For the student, Jack Burden-as-fictional-character is, then, a useful literary analogue. But, more importantly, Burden is recognizable as a human being. In the novel, Burden is a youthful, idealistic student who falls in and out of love; gets in and out of bed with his women; tries one job after another; attempts to be a scholar but finds himself being corrupted by a corrupting world; misuses his drive and energy—and so goes his youth. Many students do not know all the literary Eugene Gants, the Hamlets, or even the Hucks and Holdens who have populated the pages of our best drama and fiction. But students have no trouble recognizing Burden as "one of us." Undoubtedly his very human indecisiveness most consistently intrigues students. In Burden's tension between past and present, the present is constantly punctuated by flashbacks into the past. The past is always thoroughly idealistic: the days at Burden's Landing are captured poignantly in passage after passage.[1] "All the bright days by the water with the gulls flashing high were Anne Stanton. (p. 273)...And it was not like any summer which ever had been or was to be again." (p. 273)...That summer Adam and I would play tennis in the early morning before the sun got high and hot, and she would come to the court with us....(p. 274). "But back then there was always the afternoon. In the afternoon we always went swimming, or sailing and then swimming afterward.... Then after dinner we would get together again and sit in the shadow on their gallery or mine, or go to a movie, or take a moonlight swim..." (p. 274)

Later, of course, Burden's Landing becomes a nightmare for Jack because Anne Stanton, Adam Stanton, Judge Irwin, Jack, and everyone else changes. The naif becomes a man. His maturation process accounts for the considerable appeal which Burden-as-narrator has. This attraction is produced by the pattern woven into Burden's life: a bifurcated scheme of flight and escape into past (history) toward a belief in a deterministic world ("The Great Twitch") with a concomitant rebound into the present. Burden himself summarizes this rhythm of his life in the closing sentence of the novel: "...we shall go out of the house and go into the convulsion of the world, out of history into history and the awful responsibility of Time." (p. 438)

Burden-as-student, aside from his role as the mask of the narrator, deftly captures the spirit and mood of contemporary, evolving man in this flight pattern. His desire for knowledge, coupled with his constant hesitancy in light of the responsibility which that knowledge brings him, reflects the acute dilemma which students themselves express time and again. Numerous passages in the novel show Burden's disquietude. And the various names he gives to his fluctuation interest students, who are themselves great name makers. There is the sense of novelty and nowness in names like the Young Executive, The Scholarly Attorney, The Case of the Upright Judge, The Great Twitch, and The Great Sleeps. But perhaps the richest extended comment which engages students in finding a lot of Jack Burden in themselves is the reflective monologue early in the novel when Burden is listening to Willie Stark make a speech. This speech triggers an emotional awareness in Burden with the full impact of the dilemma he faces. Every man on the road to knowledge faces a similar upheaval. Appropriately, an organic metaphor —the embryo—expresses the trauma well. Burden reflects:

[1]Robert Penn Warren. *All the King's Men.* Bantam Books, New York, 1947. Quotations are from this edition and will be cited in the text hereafter.

It was always that way. There was the bulge and glitter, and there was
the cold grip way down in the stomach as though somebody had laid
hold of something in there, in the dark which is you, with a cold hand
in a cold rubber glove. It was like the second when you come home
late at night and see the yellow envelope of the telegram sticking out
from under your door and you lean and pick it up, but don't open it
yet, not for a second. While you stand there in the hall, with the
envelope in your hand, you feel there's an eye on you, a great big eye
looking straight at you from miles and dark and through walls and
houses and through your coat and vest and hide and sees you huddled
up way inside, in the dark which is you, inside yourself, like a clammy,
sad little foetus you carry around inside yourself. The eye knows
what's in the envelope, and it is watching you to see you when you
open it and know, too. But the clammy, sad little foetus which is you
way down in the dark which is you too lifts up its sad little face and its
eyes are blind, and it shivers cold inside you for it doesn't want to
know what is in that envelope. It wants to lie in the dark and not know,
and be warm in its not-knowing. The end of man is knowledge, but
there is one thing he can't know. He can't know whether knowledge
will save him or kill him. He will be killed, all right, but he can't
know whether he is killed because of the knowledge which he has got
or because of the knowledge which he hasn't got and which if he had it,
would save him. There's the cold in your stomach, but you open the
envelope, you have to open the envelope, for the end of man is to know.

(p. 9)

I have dwelt this long on Burden-as-human rather than Burden-
as-fictive-device because students do not really care about all the
literary analogues ultimately, especially not today's students. But
whenever the occasion arises, it is useful to exploit Warren's sophis-
tication by pointing out the literary allusions: there is the title
(which is not a simple nursery rhyme echo, it turns out, once you
start explicating its meaning): or the Dantean epigraph on the title
page; and there are other literary devices which shed a good deal of
light on the total picture of the complexity of Warren's narrator. For
instance, the Dantean motif gives Burden's outlook a rather different cast—an optimistic one—which one sees more precisely by ex-
ploring the context of the quotation from *The Divine Comedy*.[2] For
despite his escapist attitudes evident in many scenes in the novel,
Burden finally does come to grips with his own personality. What
he sees is a radically modified determinism, colored by a corrected
vision of his own role in shaping his destiny. He does not conclude

[2]See my explication of the epigraph in *Explicator*, XVII (December 1967), Item
29.

on a totally optimistic note, but he does more clearly know what effect he can have in shaping his own end. The rebirth and conversion motifs are prominent in the novel, and these leitmotifs are worth bringing to students' attention also in relation to these continuing revelations which Burden has about himself. As students say, this qualified determinism is about all anyone could ask for. Every teacher now sees that today's student has changed his question from a teleological *why* to a psychological *how*. The question is not *did* Humpty Dumpty fall, or *why* did he fall, or even why do things in general fall apart. But *how* are they to be put back together again. The young soldier returning home from Vietnam, the black student returning to the ghetto from a college education, the WASP grappling with the implications of his history—all of today's children want to know *how* to put it back together again. They all know you can't go home again, but they will keep on trying. And they know Burden's solution is not simple, not even entirely clear. But his formulation, his articulation of a plan holds some promise. Students in today's classrooms are aware of themselves in a historical context, and they are hellbent on finding answers to questions they have about their past, present, and future.

For many readers of *All the King's Men* the more intriguing character is not Jack Burden, but Willie Stark. Such a reading inevitably points toward the Huey Long saga as background for the novel. Warren has told rather fully (and somewhat ambiguously) why the novel is not "about" Long; and, after all, one feels inclined to let the novelist's explanation stand.[3] Yet certain parallels between Willie Stark and Huey Long are obvious, and any study of the novel without a nod toward these parallels is shortsighted. Some recent biographies of Long are especially useful in getting at the Long legend, as historians, political scientists, and others continue to find the Long era an engaging aspect of Americana. Exploiting the Stark-Long analogies is, however, for the short run; in the long run, Stark's role in the novel offers a more extended insight only in its primary relation to Jack Burden. Stark helps Burden reflect, redefine, and rediscover himself.

Willie Stark (as his name also signals) is a man of stark fact. He contrasts sharply with Adam Stanton, the "man of idea," as Burden calls him. These categories are partly ironic, of course, because they

[3]Warren has commented on the background of the novel at least twice in periodicals. See his explanation in "A Note on *All the King's Men,*" *Sewanee Review* (Summer, 1953) and *"All the King's Men:* The Matrix of Experience," *Yale Review,* LIII (December 1963), 161-167.

are indeed aspects of Burden's own personality. For it is Burden who gives himself fully to his research—the facts—whenever the Boss wants him to do so. And only when the "dirt" rubs off on Burden's own past, his own father and mother, does his idealism become tarnished.[4] The man of fact in the society of the 70's has not as much going for him as he had in the immediate past, even as recently as the 60's. As originally conceived, Warren says that Willie Stark and Stanton were to represent the scientists of our world. Thus the curious blending of the fact-ideal world in the two closest friends of Burden presents a tension which modern students with a science-humanism orientation find themselves grappling with more and more. Burden's own tensions are mirrored in the conflict between his two friends. Perhaps Stark is finally important to us because we recognize him for his Machiavellian demogoguery.

This is not the place to list the Machiavellian demogogues that have traipsed across the stage of our little world, but undoubtedly some of the American Machiavels are recognizable enough to be painful for Americans. For notorious reasons, Southern politicians seem to bear the brunt of comparison when Stark's machinations are analyzed. And the Long dynasty in Louisiana obviously makes a comfortable parallel. Furthermore, Robert Penn Warren is by birth and some training a Southerner; and there is no little interest in this biographical fact since all of his novels have a Southern setting. (This despite the fact that Warren long ago gave up making the mint julep for making mint of the Ft. Knox variety.) Nevertheless, Willie's Machiavellian roots yield some intriguing revelations for historians and young political scientists in the classroom. What more incisive method of seeing machine politics and the Mafia orientation of today's political scene than through the philosophy of Willie Stark. Here rolled up into a neat ball is William James' pragmatism and a set of deep south godfathers long before Talese or Puzo.

Stark's philosophy is best seen in the action of the novel, for he is, after all, a man of action—not idea. (This itself is a provocative concept of the political panorama today.) But succinctly put, Stark's view of the world, God, and man boils down to an aphoristically-sounding doctrine echoing the pragmatic philosophy which guides him for good or for evil: "Man is conceived in sin and born in cor-

[4]In true Hollywood fashion, when *All the King's Men* was made into a movie, Broderick Crawford, who played the role of Stark was the star who won the Oscar. John Ireland, who played the role of Burden was a secondary character. Ironically, Hollywood gave Burden a kind of anti-heroic position, the ultimate role he assumes in the novel.

ruption and he passeth from the stink of the didie to the stench of the shroud. There is always something." (p. 157) The sardonic wit of Burden always filters our impressions of Stark, and one supposes that Stark is really worse than the naive Burden ever sees him, until it is almost too late. But Stark is not only the political manipulator, the Jacobean Machiavel: before the bloody Sunday ending of the novel, the entire political set-up is brought into sharp focus. The "Case of the Upright Judge" is the label Burden puts on his "excursion" into the past. And in that past the taintless Governor Stanton, Judge Irwin, and all the other "pure hearts, clean hands" souls are tarnished through and through. And so that we understand the inevitable link between the past and the present, Burden's ancestors, the Masterns, are shown for their own special brand of manipulation. Wherever he turns, Jack Burden's ultimate education is his understanding that all of life is political. Structurally, the Cass Mastern episode fills a neat intercalary place in Burden's education. Jack accurately links the Masterns' life with the Case of the Upright Judge, and from both cases Jack learns a lesson he tries desperately to avoid. He learns that: "...the world is all of one piece...that the world is like an enormous spider web and if you touch it, however lightly, at any point, the vibration ripples to the remotest perimeter and the drowsy spider feels the tingle and is drowsy no more.... It does not matter whether or not you meant to brush the web of things. Your happy foot or your gay wing may have brushed it ever so lightly, but what happens always happens...." (pp. 188-189). The escape into a deterministic epistemology no longer works for Burden, though he avoids even this admission until much later:

> But later, much later, he woke up one morning to discover that he did not believe in the Great Twitch any more. He did not believe in it because he had seen too many people live and die. He had seen Lucy Stark and Sugar-Boy and the Scholarly Attorney and Sadie Burke and Anne Stanton live and the ways of their living had nothing to do with the Great Twitch. He had seen his father die. He had seen his friend Adam Stanton die. He had seen his friend Willie Stark die....
> (p. 436)

The ultimate significance, then, for the historian or political scientist in a study of *All the King's Men* is not in finding the Machiavellian parallels in the novel, but in showing how these aspects of the novel shed light on the progressive revelations the political events make on the protagonist, Jack Burden. Warren is not, furthermore, satirizing Southern politics; he is not asserting that political action is impossible in an individual with deep personal integrity: and he is not suggesting that a Calvinistic view of man is the most pragmatic approach to understanding how the modern political state operates. Too many people (notably Hugh Miller and Jack Burden himself) contradict these false assumptions which some historians and political scientists have drawn from the novel. Miller and Burden do return to the political arena, and we are left with a far more moral world than we began with in the novel.[5] If the novel shows us anything then from an historical perspective it is that easy generalizations about the nature of man as political animal are likely to be misleading. Burden learns this lesson through much pain and suffering.

The strengths of *All the King's Men* as a teachable piece of fiction rest primarily in the implications of these two areas which I have explored here in a cursory manner: with Burden as an Everyman archetype and in the power politics of Willie Stark. I have only sketched these two aspects rather than overlisting examples from the novel and from contemporary events for illustration. Students make discoveries for themselves concerning both the role of Jack Burden and the political implications. Depending on the level of maturity of the student, these discoveries may be rather simple, or they may be profound. In teaching this novel for more than ten years, I have also found some of the following exercises fruitful:

1. Considering the overall philosophical implications of suffering in the novel, what kind of case can be made for Jack Burden as Job? What about the similarity in the initials? Trace the Biblical parallels and allusions to Biblical figures throughout the novel.

2. How is Jack Burden an existential hero? Is he an anti-hero? Considering Robert P. Warren's classical education at Vanderbilt and his disclosures about his reading in the ancients during composition of the original play (upon which the novel is based), what kind of hero has Warren created?

3. What is the role of sports and athletics in the novel? One notices, for example, several remarks and indeed extended passages about swimming, hunting, fishing, football, tennis, and so forth.

4. Turn to the facts of Robert Penn Warren's life and consider his contributions to the Agrarian movement in American literature, particularly *I'll Take My Stand*. What implications are there in the facts of Warren's early writings, including *All the King's Men*, and his

[5]I am indebted to Seymour L. Gross for his insights on this point. See his "The Achievement of Robert Penn Warren," *College English XIX* (May 1958), 361-365.

recent attitudes toward civil rights? Is there significance in the fact that no blacks appear in *All the King's Men*?

5. Pursuing the symbolic function of various aspects of the novel, consider the following: the eye imagery; the Dantean epigraph; the title; the rebirth imagery; uses of water and sunlight.

6. Even though, for the most part, the narrator is sombre and philosophically introspective, there are great bursts of humor laced throughout. Example: "You could hear one insane and irrelevant July fly sawing away up in one of the catalpa trees in the square." (p. 9) Or, "No," the Boss said, getting ready again to turn around, "and I don't care if it was the sainted uncut maiden aunt of the Apostle Paul." (p. 20) Or, "The gang of us sat around and moved our thighs on the horse hair...and stared down at the unpainted boards of the floor... as though we were attending a funeral and owed the dead man some money." (p. 24). What is the function of these humorous passages? Satiric? Sardonic? Comic relief? (Note when the passages occur.)

7. Warren says he did not want to write a "straight naturalistic novel" in planning the book. What is a "straight naturalistic novel," and what is the difference in [sic] that kind of book and this novel?

8. *Proud Flesh* is the title of the original play that became the novel, *All the King's Men*. Read the play and Warren's comments about it; then discuss what has taken place in the artistic process.

9. The prefrontal lobectomy which Adam Stanton performs on a patient is in miniature the process of Jack Burden's own transformation of personality. Examine the similarities and differences.

10. Consider the novel as tragedy. What are the relationships between the tragic aspects of this novel and classical tragedy? Consider the role of fate (i.e. determinism, "The Great Twitch") versus free will as the basic ingredient in both kinds of tragedy. How does the violence motif which undergirds so much of the action relate to the contemporary fascination with violence in American movies and television?

Too many claims for greatness have been made for too many works of fiction. A claim of uniqueness for Warren's *All the King's Men* is not the intention here. Not all readers find the novel as richly humorous, as politically exciting, or as totally pertinent to humanity as I have tried to suggest. In a final analysis, the novel resists categorizing, becoming *sui generis* since it depicts many complex matters simultaneously. But above all, the novel does go a long way toward fulfilling William Faulkner's hints about the worthiness of modern authors to fulfill their function in our time. In the Nobel Prize Speech, Faulkner suggested that writers today must continue to write about "the problems of the human heart in conflict with itself which alone can make good writing because only that is worth writing about, worth the agony and the sweat." *All the King's Men* succeeds best in the classroom when one has time enough to explore more precisely how the characters, the plot, structure, tone, symbolism—indeed all of these and other elements blend into a pattern. When the multiple themes in the novel are unravelled and made pertinent to modern man, the dimensions of the novel as a work of art begin to unfold.

After all these analyses have been drawn between the novel and life itself, I detect that one important—even overriding aspect of this book often goes unnoted. The novel is finally about the power of love in the universe to change a man. Warren hints at this in the Dantean epigraph, and he develops this theme in several ways throughout the novel. As a love story with far richer impact than the brand offered in Segal's best seller, the novel makes an important comment. Jack Burden serves as the catalyst in the objective correlative: he sees, records, and though trying not to, he reacts to his impressions. All of the "love affairs" (Jack's, Willie's, Anne's, Jack's mother's, and others) eventually amount to far more than all the political affairs. Some critics have urged that the novel ends on a sentimental note, that the essential comic ending is too easy, even weak. Perhaps one should argue that it is difficult for calloused moderns to accept readily that the power of love in the universe does radically alter the lives of those who experience it. Jack Burden learns that he has instinctively loved Judge Irwin, though Burden does not know why until long after he discovers that the Judge is his real father. Burden learns to love his mother, whom he has thoroughly despised previously. Burden finally forgives and accepts Anne with all her blemishes, knowing that she too suffers from the deep hurt resulting from her life with Willie and the unmasking of her father's life. Even the Scholarly Attorney takes on a new attraction for Burden, who finally consoles the old man in the face of imminent death. This newest role for Jack is an entirely different one, a sympathetic, compassionate sensitivity brought about by his Damascus-like conversion foreshadowed throughout the book. Popular lyrics of today's songs suggest that what the world needs now is love, love, love. If the novel ends unfashionably tame, one must remember that the comedy envisioned by Dante was a *divine* comedy. Warren is not depicting a Christian medieval world view, but he is suggesting a thoroughly moral universe. A world devoid of love, Warren seems to say, is as chaotic, as purposeless, as irreconcilable as it was before man entered it. (Warren draws the same conclusion in his most recent novel, *Meet Me in the Green Glen.*)* This is man's world, and man controls his destiny, and he can "put it back together again" if it seems to fall apart. The novel is not a program for reform nor an apology for an ethical system to discover precisely how man reassembles Humpty Dumpty. But the novel does assert that so long as Eternal Love exists man can be redeemed. Who could ask for anything more.

*[Warren has since completed his tenth novel, *A Place to Come To* (1977). — Ed.]

Chronology of Important Dates

	Warren	The Age
1905	Born (April 24), Guthrie, Kentucky.	
1914		World War I begins.
1918		Armistice signed.
1921	Graduates from Clarksville, Tennessee, high school and enters Vanderbilt University.	
1922		T. S. Eliot, "The Waste Land"; James Joyce, *Ulysses*.
1923	Joins Nashville "Fugitive" group.	
1925	Graduates *summa cum laude* from Vanderbilt; begins graduate study in English at University of California (MA, 1927).	John T. Scopes found guilty of teaching evolution in Dayton, Tennessee; F. Scott Fitzgerald, *The Great Gatsby*.
1926		Ernest Hemingway, *The Sun Also Rises*.
1927	Graduate study in English at Yale University.	Lindbergh flight from New York to Paris.
1928	Rhodes Scholar, Oxford University (B. Litt., 1930).	
1929	*John Brown: The Making of a Martyr*.	Stock Market Crash begins Depression; William Faulkner, *The Sound and the Fury;* Hemingway, *A Farewell to Arms;* Thomas Wolfe, *Look Homeward, Angel*.
1930	*I'll Take My Stand* by "Twelve Southerners"; marries Emma Brescia; assistant professor of English, Southwestern College, Memphis.	Sinclair Lewis becomes first American to win Nobel Prize for Literature.

1931	Assistant professor of English, Vanderbilt.	
1932		Franklin D. Roosevelt elected to first term as President.
1934	Assistant professor of English, Louisiana State University.	Hitler becomes German Fuehrer; Mao Tse-Tung and Chinese Communists begin Long March; Fitzgerald, *Tender Is The Night.*
1935	*Approach to Literature* (with Cleanth Brooks and John T. Purser); *Thirty-Six Poems;* founds *The Southern Review* (with Brooks and Charles W. Pipkin).	Governor Huey P. Long assassinated in Louisiana State Capitol (September 8).
1936	Associate professor, LSU.	Civil War begins in Spain; Faulkner, *Absalom, Absalom!*
1938	*Understanding Poetry* (with Brooks).	Allen Tate, *The Fathers.*
1939	*Night Rider;* awarded first Guggenheim Fellowship.	World War II begins in Europe.
1941		Japanese attack Pearl Harbor and U.S. enters War.
1942	*Eleven Poems on the Same Theme:* Professor of English, University of Minnesota.	
1943	*At Heaven's Gate; Understanding Fiction* (with Brooks).	
1944	*Selected Poems 1923-1943;* occupies Poetry Chair, Library of Congress.	
1945		Roosevelt dies and Harry S. Truman becomes President; atomic bombs dropped on Japan; World War II ends.
1946	*All the King's Men* (Pulitzer Prize).	Cold War begins; Nuremberg Trials.
1947	Awarded second Guggenheim Fellowship.	

1948	*The Circus in the Attic and Other Stories.*	
1950	*World Enough and Time;* Professor of Playwriting, Yale Drama School.	Faulkner wins Nobel Prize; Korean War begins.
1951	Divorces Emma Brescia.	
1952	Marries Eleanor Clark. Elected to American Philosophical Society.	Dwight D. Eisenhower elected President.
1953	*Brother to Dragons: A Tale in Verse and Voices.*	Korean War ends.
1954		Supreme Court school desegregation decision; Army-McCarthy hearings.
1955	*Band of Angels.*	Montgomery, Alabama bus boycott.
1957	*Promises: Poems 1954-1956* (Pulitzer Prize, National Book Award); *Segregation: The Inner Conflict in the South.*	Sputnik I launched by USSR.
1958	*Selected Essays: Remember the Alamo!* (children's book).	
1959	*The Cave;* election to The American Academy of Arts and and Letters.	Fidel Castro assumes power in Cuba.
1960	*You, Emperors, and Others: Poems 1957-1960; All the King's Men* (play).	John F. Kennedy elected President; civil rights "sit-ins" in South.
1961	*Wilderness; The Legacy of the Civil War;* professor of English, Yale.	"Bay of Pigs" invasion; first American troops sent to Vietnam.
1962		Cuban missile crisis.
1963		President Kennedy assassinated; Lyndon Johnson becomes president.
1964	*Flood: A Romance of Our Time.*	

1965	*Who Speaks for the Negro?*	Malcolm X assassinated; Selma to Montgomery, Alabama, civil rights march; riots in Watts area of Los Angeles.
1966	*Selected Poems: New and Old, 1923-1966.*	U.S. bombs Hanoi to escalate Vietnam War.
1967	Awarded Bollingen Prize in Poetry.	Six-day Israeli-Arab War.
1968	*Incarnations: Poems 1966-1968.*	Tet offensive in Vietnam; Robert F. Kennedy assassinated; Martin Luther King, Jr., assassinated.
1969	*Audubon: A Vision.*	Astronaut Neil Armstrong walks on moon; Richard M. Nixon becomes president.
1970	*Selected Poems of Herman Melville;* awarded National Medal for Literature.	President Nixon orders Cambodian "incursion."
1971	*Meet Me in the Green Glen; John Greenleaf Whittier's Poetry; Homage to Theodore Drieser.*	"Pentagon Papers" published.
1972		President Nixon goes to China prior to re-election; Alabama Governor George Wallace shot while campaigning; Watergate break-in.
1973	*Ámerican Literature: The Makers and the Making* (with Cleanth Brooks and R. W. B. Lewis).	Vice President Spiro Agnew resigns; Senate Watergate hearings.
1974	*Or Else—Poem/ Poems 1968-1974;* delivers third annual Jefferson Lecture in the Humanities.	President Nixon resigns; Gerald Ford becomes president.
1975	*Democracy and Poetry* (1974 Jefferson Lecture).	Last American troops leave Vietnam.
1976	*Selected Poems: 1923-1975.*	Jimmy Carter elected president.
1977	*A Place to Come To.*	

Notes on the Editor and Contributors

ROBERT H. CHAMBERS, the editor, has taught at Brown and Yale Universities and is now Dean of the College of Arts and Sciences and Associate Professor of English at Bucknell University. He is currently completing a full-length study on Robert Penn Warren.

JONATHAN BAUMBACH is Professor of English at Brooklyn College and Co-Director of the MFA Program in Creative Writing. In addition to *The Landscape of Nightmare* (1965), he has published seven books, including four novels.

BEEKMAN W. COTTRELL, Professor and Director of Undergraduate Studies in the English department at Carnegie-Mellon University, has published essays on Faulkner, Warren, Shakespeare, and Graham Greene, and edited several volumes in Noble's Insight Series.

NORTON R. GIRAULT, an officer in the U. S. Navy for more than twenty years, now writes poetry and fiction and teaches English at Norfolk State College in Virginia.

ROBERT B. HEILMAN, Professor of English at the University of Washington and twice a Guggenheim Fellow, has written and edited many volumes, including *The Ghost on the Ramparts and Other Essays in the Humanities* (1973) and (with Cleanth Brooks) *Understanding Drama* (1948).

JEROME MECKIER, author of *Aldous Huxley: Satire and Structure* (1969) and of articles on T. S. Eliot, Evelyn Waugh, and others, is Professor of English and Director of Graduate Study at the University of Kentucky.

LADELL PAYNE, Professor of English and Chairman of the Department of Literature and Languages at Claremont Men's College, has published several essays on Southern writers as well as the book *Thomas Wolfe* (1969).

JAMES RUOFF, whose most recent books include *Major Elizabethan Poetry and Prose* (1972) and *Crowell's Handbook of Elizabethan and Stuart Literature* (1975), is Professor of English at City College of the City University of New York.

JAMES C. SIMMONS, author of *The Novelist as Historian: Essays on the Victorian Historical Novel* (1973), combines part-time teaching at San Diego State University with free-lance work as a travel writer, lecturer, and photographer.

ROBERT C. SLACK, Professor of English at Carnegie-Mellon University, is the editor of *Bibliographies of Studies in Victorian Literature* (1967) and co-author (with Beekman W. Cottrell) of *Write On: A Preparation for College Composition* (1971).

ROBERT PENN WARREN, author of *All the King's Men,* recently retired from teaching at Yale and has just published his tenth novel, *A Place to Come To.*

EARL J. WILCOX, Chairman of the Department of English, Drama at Winthrop College in South Carolina, is co-author (with David L. Rankin) of *Fundamentals of Fiction* (1975) and has published articles on Jack London, Poe, Twain, Hemingway, and others.

Selected Bibliography

Bentley, Eric. "The Meaning of Robert Penn Warren's Novels." *The Kenyon Review.* 10, no. 3 (Summer 1948): 407-24. "Warren is a faulty writer (but) he is worth a dozen petty perfectionists. Though commonly associated with 'formalists' and 'classicists' in criticism, he is close to the type of romantic genius: robust, fluent, versatile, at his worst clever and clumsy, at his best brilliant and profound."

Eisinger, Chester E. *Fiction of the Forties* (Chicago: University of Chicago Press, 1963), pp. 214-23. "No writer in our time except Faulkner has given us a book that speaks so eloquently with a conservative voice.'"

Gross, Seymour L. "Conrad and *All the King's Men.*" *Twentieth Century Literature* 3 no. 1 (April 1957): 27-32. "Warren's finest novel owes even more to Conrad's *Heart of Darkness* than does Fitzgerald's *The Great Gatsby.*"

Justus, James H. "All the Burdens of Warren's *All the King's Men,*" in *The Forties: Fiction, Poetry, Drama,* edited by Warren French (Deland, Florida: Everett Edwards, Inc., 1969), pp. 191-201. "Although Burden reconstructs his own past with as much detachment as he does the entire context of the Stark era, he still bears the personal marks of that ordeal."

Kaplan, Charles. "Jack Burden: Modern Ishmael," *College English* 22, no. 1 (October 1960): 19-24. "Ishmael and Jack Burden recreate...an archetypal pattern of human behavior, moving, as Aristotle has it, from ignorance to knowledge...or from isolation to common cause with mankind."

Mizener, Arthur. "Robert Penn Warren: *All the King's Men.*" *The Southern Review* 3 new series. no. 4 (October 1967): 874-94. "...in the confrontation of its two central characters, *All the King's Men* poses what is for Mr. Warren the central problem of existence, the irrepressible conflict between the conception of life that gives action meaning and value and the act of living in the world in which meaning and value have to be realized."

Rubin, Louis D., Jr. *The Faraway Country: Writers of the Modern South* (Seattle: University of Washington Press, 1963), pp. 105-30. In the "particular relationship between Jack Burden...and the place in which he was born and grew up can be found a highly revealing commentary about modern Southern experience."

Sillars, Malcolm O. "Warren's *All the King's Men:* A Study in Populism." *American Quarterly* 9 no. 3 (Fall 1957): 345-53. "...all the king's men, and the king himself, can be clearly seen to represent the great American tradition of Populism that swept the poorer agricultural areas of the Middle West and the South in the late 1930's."

Strout, Cushing. "*All the King's Men* and the Shadow of William James." *The Southern Review* 6, new series, no. 4 (October 1970): 920-34. "Warren's novel...is...a dramatic exploration of the major themes of James's philosophy."

Warren, Robert Penn. '*All the King's Men*: The Matrix of Experience." *The Yale Review* 53, no. 2 (December 1963): 161-67. "What Louisiana and Senator Long gave me was a line of thinking and feeling that did eventuate in the novel."